Praise from People Who Have Learned These Techniques

Are you crazy? Smile to my organs? Talk to them? No way! I was a typical Westerner, all in my head, until I got lung cancer and lost a lung. Out of desperation, I started to smile and talk to and love my other lung and all my inner organs. By God, it works! I learned to love my organs as much as I love my cat, which is a lot. Now, I converse and smile to my dear organs every day. Only 4 percent survive lung cancer; my organs are keeping me alive. I *really love* them — they're my inner family.

H., lung cancer survivor

The Sounds and Inner Smile have been extremely valuable for my spiritual growth and my everyday life. Two surprising benefits are: better focus and ability to relax during my golf competitions, and letting go of old resentments, especially of my mother-in-law.

D., retired businesswoman

I have so many choices to make every day that it can be very stressful. After I do the Healing Sounds, it's easy. The right choices are clear.

R., college student

My five-year-old daughter and I do the Healing Sounds together. She loves them, and they calm her down before bedtime. When our baby is fussy, my wife holds him on her lap and does the *HEEEEEE* sound, and he settles down.

D., filmmaker

Practicing the Healing Sounds offers me an escape valve for the built-up emotions that can clog the body and create chronic disease.

B., acupuncturist

When I do the Six Sounds, I feel balanced and together throughout the day and week. Negative situations don't throw me off balance.

G., database administrator

I had insomnia for six months. Doing the Six Healing Sounds for twenty minutes before sleeping helped me have sound sleep.

T., chiropractor

I had poor digestion for years. I've been doing the Sounds and Inner Smile for a few months now, and I'm happy to say my digestion is actually good.

C., teacher

My bowels have worked much better since I've been doing the Healing Sounds regularly.

B., labor organizer

The Inner Smile has brought such a radiance to my whole being. I feel such love and gratitude for each part of my body. This practice has heightened my awareness of the beauty and joy in my life experiences.

L., musician, artist

In the morning, before I get out of bed, I imagine myself standing at the foot of the bed, smiling lovingly at me. I use that loving energy to do the Inner Smile. Then, in the shower, I do the Six Healing Sounds. I wash out the old and bring in the new energy. After I do these two practices, I'm filled with happy energy, and my emotions stay balanced throughout the day.

A., physical therapist

EMOTIONAL
WISDOM

EMOTIONAL WISDOM

Daily Tools for Transforming
Anger, Depression,
and Fear

Mantak Chia
and Dena Saxer

New World Library
Novato, California

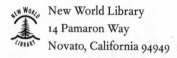

New World Library
14 Pamaron Way
Novato, California 94949

Text design by Tona Pearce Myers
Interior photographs by Fae Horowitz

ISBN-13: 978-1-57731-612-1

Printed in the U.S.A.

CAUTION

If you are currently experiencing a severe emotional crisis, or you have unresolved emotional traumas from the past, we urge you to work on your issues with a skilled therapist, counselor, or spiritual advisor.

The techniques in this book are safe and effective for ordinary, mild emotional stresses. However, severe crises or deep-seated traumas may be aggravated by relying on these techniques alone without professional treatment or guidance.

All recommendations given in our book are based on the ancient Chinese teachings of chi kung (qigong) and Traditional Chinese Medicine, as well as on our own experience, intuition, and research. As always, *your own* experience, intuition, and research are the best and final guide to what works for you.

To deepen your use and understanding of the tools in this book, or to learn more advanced chi kung methods, you can locate a trained and certified Universal Healing Tao instructor in your area at http://directoryofuniversaltaoinstructors.com/.

Mantak Chia's website is www.universal-tao.com.
Dena Saxer's website is www.universaltaola.com.

CONTENTS

INTRODUCTION

The Need for Transforming Our Painful Emotions

OUR SOCIETY IS EMOTIONALLY DISABLED. According to statistics from the National Institute of Mental Health for 2005, every year one in four Americans age eighteen or older suffers from a "diagnosable mental disorder." Considering the present economic recession, the current number of people with mental disorders is likely greater. The NIMH list of mental disorders includes depression, bipolar disorder, anxiety disorders, phobias, post-traumatic stress disorder, obsessive-compulsive disorder, eating disorders, and suicide. Even many adults who have no discernible emotional disorders feel stressed out by the complexities, pressures, and uncertainties of modern life. Clearly, there's a need for practical and accessible tools for emotional health.

Emotional Wisdom presents a powerful self-healing program that transforms the painful emotions of anger, depression, fear, and guilt into kindness, courage, joy, and peacefulness. Our book presents three clear, easy ten- or twenty-minute Taoist practices with step-by-step directions and helpful illustrations that will allow you to guide your-self through the techniques. The first two practices, the Six Healing Sounds and the Inner Smile, have been used for over two thousand years in China. The third practice, Releasing One Emotion, is our unique extension of the other two. All three are forms of chi kung. *Chi* means "energy" or "breath." *Kung* means "skilled practice or disci-pline." Chi kung means cultivating life-force energy: refining it, increasing it, directing it, and raising its vibration.

Our Western Problem with "Negative" Emotions

Most of us in Western society are not taught how to deal effectively with our so-called negative emotions. Some people act out their anger, frustration, or cruelty directly — by harming others verbally or physically. Most of us regard negative emotions as weaknesses, character flaws, or even sins. As civilized people, we're taught to reject them — to hide, deny, or repress their existence, to train our-selves not to feel these disturbing energies. Of course, they don't go away. They keep building up; they embed themselves in our internal organs, our muscles, and our psyche. Sometimes, they break out and embarrass us — in a sudden fit of anger — or they take the form of an unexpected bout of depression or excessive worry. They sabotage our lives, creating neuroses, addictions, and physical diseases. And by silencing our natural responses to negative emotions, we silence our natural responses to the positive emotions as well. Life may look good on the surface, but in truth we feel hollow and meaningless. Life without passion is a living death.

Taoism: All Emotions Are Natural

Taoism, the five-thousand-year-old Chinese philosophy of life — along with its branches, chi kung (qigong) and Traditional Chinese

Medicine (TCM) — has a different view of painful emotions. All emotions are seen as forms of energy, and they're accepted as natural expressions of our human life. The seemingly negative emotions are *valuable messages from our Soul*; they're telling us that something is out of balance and needs to be changed. Taoism recognizes that unresolved negative emotions are harmful, but this is not because they're bad or sinful.

Western medicine regards bacteria and viruses as primary causes of disease. In contrast, Traditional Chinese Medicine sees imbalances of body, mind, or Spirit as the primary causes of disease; bacteria and viruses affect only people already weakened by emotional or physical imbalances. TCM divides the causes of disease into three categories: internal, external, and other.

In Chinese medicine, the *primary internal cause of disease* is emotional disharmony. Holding on to anger, sadness, fear, or worry, or variations of these, stresses a corresponding pair of internal organs. This causes those organs to malfunction and become diseased. Please note that chi kung and TCM recognize that each internal organ has a wide area of influence through its meridian (an energy pathway), its relationship to all the other organs and their meridians, and its specific spiritual function. If negative emotions continue to build up in a particular organ, without being transformed, eventually the surrounding blood, muscles, tendons, and other internal organs are also harmed.

In TCM, *external causes of disease* are results of extremes of climate: excessive heat, cold, wind, dampness, or dryness. An excess of air-conditioning or dry central heating can also cause disease.

Other causes of disease besides internal and external are a weak constitution, physical or mental overexertion, excessive sexual activity, a poor diet, trauma, parasites, poisons, and incorrect medical treatment.[1]

Painful emotions also disturb our blood's pH balance, the ratio of alkalinity to acidity. Our blood becomes thicker and acidic, and so it moves more slowly and works less effectively. Acidic blood makes us more susceptible to infection and illness.

On a spiritual level, negativity blocks our progress. The Taoist solution is to learn from and harness the powerful energies of troubling emotions by transmuting them into positive life-force energy. In this way, the toxins of our lives become the medicines for our rejuvenation, relaxation, and spiritual development.

Recent Western Acceptance of Eastern Wisdom

Western medicine and psychology are now validating the ancient Taoist wisdom and practices. Scientists are studying and acknowledging the destructive effect of long-held painful emotions. A new specialty in psychosomatic medicine, psychoneuroimmunology (also called psychoimmunology), was created in 1975. It studies the interaction between emotional states and the immune system. Its basic premise is that the body and mind are inseparable. Neuroscientist Candace Pert's studies demonstrate that all emotions are biochemical reactions that can harm or heal the body. The popular film *What the Bleep Do We Know!?* dramatizes and illustrates some of her findings.

In recent years, some allopathic doctors (MDs) and insurance companies have begun using an "integrative medicine" approach — that is, working in tandem with doctors of Oriental medicine, acupuncturists, and Chinese herbalists. The network of medical practitioners associated with the University of Southern California, Los Angeles, now includes the UCLA Center for East-West Medicine, which offers acupuncture, acupressure, and trigger-point injections that are covered by some insurance plans. The UCLA network also periodically offers free classes and lectures in meditation. Many MDs and insurance companies now recommend that their patients take classes in stress reduction, anger management, meditation, hatha yoga, tai chi, and chi kung to improve their mental and physical health. These methods can be of enormous benefit.

The Six Healing Sounds and the Inner Smile can be catalysts that complement other methods of therapy, or they can stand on their own. When we do them regularly, we improve all areas of our lives.

Description of the Emotional Wisdom Tools

The Six Healing Sounds practice uses specific sounds, arm movements, and visualized colors to release negative emotions from, and correct physical imbalances in, particular internal organs. For example, unresolved anger makes its home in the liver and gallbladder. To release anger, we focus our attention on our liver and ask it for the message of the anger or other imbalance we are experiencing. The message may come immediately or at a later time. Then we say the sound *SHHHHHH* (the sound used to request quiet) with the appropriate arm movement, and we visualize anger as a cloudy gray substance being released into the ground. Next, we visualize green light flooding our liver, which changes the anger to kindness. Simultaneously, this technique relaxes and energizes the liver and gallbladder. We repeat each sound and arm movement three to six times. Doing all six sounds in a time-tested order balances the temperature and energy of our entire body, gives us greater focus and grounding, calms and relaxes us, and improves our physical health. Our happiness increases exponentially!

Our version of the Six Healing Sounds preserves 100 percent of the ancient practice as taught to Mantak Chia at age fifteen by his Chinese master teacher, Yi Eng, in Hong Kong. Mantak Chia has enhanced the practice by adding details from Traditional Chinese Medicine: corresponding emotions and psychological traits, colors, and seasons. He also added placing one's hands on the body over the corresponding organs. From Western anatomy, he has added descriptions of the functions of the internal organs. Based on her intuition, Dena added asking for the message of the negative emotion and seeing the color as colored light. These innovations make the Six Healing Sounds a more profound experience — and they fit the Taoist principle of continual change.

In part II of this book, Emotions — Messages from Our Soul, we offer our personal interpretations of the valuable messages of anger, depression, fear, worry, hate, and their variations. Then, based on chi kung and Traditional Chinese Medicine teachings, we identify the specific internal organs that are adversely affected when each of these emotions is not released or transformed. We also recommend particular colors and tastes of food that alleviate specific painful emotions and support corresponding positive emotions.

The Inner Smile practice begins with visualizing and feeling a joyful image in our mind's eye; we then move that "smiling energy" into the brain, the heart, the internal organs, and the spine, thanking each part of our body for its particular function as we go. This technique fosters appreciation and gratitude for our marvelous human body. It also improves our self-esteem by consciously reprogramming us to love ourselves inwardly and outwardly. As a result, we have more love for others. We then attract more positive people and more desirable events in our lives. The Inner Smile is simple, yet so profound.

Our version of the Inner Smile preserves 100 percent of the ancient practice as taught by Yi Eng. Mantak Chia added more explanation of the functions of the organs, and he organized the sequence into three logical lines. These changes deepen the experience and make it easier to remember the steps.

Dena designed the Releasing One Emotion practice, which adds a step for individual, deep-seated painful emotions. In this practice we examine one emotion at a time, deepen and exaggerate its feeling, release it physically, and ask for the lesson of the emotion. The practice concludes with forgiveness for all concerned, including ourselves. She and her students have had good results with this technique.

The last part of the book is called "Taoist Natural First Aid: Physical Healing." It offers specific sounds and dietary advice for relieving common minor physical symptoms, which are listed alphabetically.

Practical Spirituality

All spiritual systems emphasize the importance of cultivating the virtues of kindness, patience, compassion, and agape, or unconditional love. But very few books give us concise, accessible formulas for releasing the toxins of anger, sadness, fear, or anxiety. *Emotional Wisdom*'s ten- to twenty-minute, easily grasped techniques release and transform turbulent emotions into an immediate sense of calm and balance. Practicing them puts the tools of transformation in our own hands — power tools for recycling our emotional baggage into vitality, joy, and inner peace.

For thousands of years, chi kung and Chinese medicine have taught that clinging to negative emotions is the *primary* internal cause of disease. And they have advocated the use of tai chi, chi kung postures, and meditation, as well as a balanced diet, to prevent disease and support healing. The old-fashioned classical Chinese doctor was paid to help families prevent illness; he visited and checked each family regularly and was paid monthly. He was not paid when they were ill.

As we do the Healing Sounds and Inner Smile, and as we transform our emotions, our physical health improves. Our internal
organs become stronger and more efficient. We're also able to alleviate specific physical symptoms such as headaches, sore throat, colds,
indigestion, insomnia, and many others by doing a relevant sound
and then smiling into the area of discomfort. This is multitasking at
its best.

Suggestions for Using This Book

This is primarily a practical workbook; its value depends on how you
use it. It's organized so that each section builds on the previous one.
The first two chapters contain explanations that enhance and deepen
the effect of the three major tools for transforming troubling emotions. However, as always, follow your intuition. You could start by
doing just one Healing Sound or the first line of the Inner Smile.
Then we recommend that, after sampling one of the practices, you go
back and digest each section in the given order. It's best to thoroughly
learn and practice one of the three tools for Emotional Wisdom at a
time. Allow yourself a few weeks to memorize and feel comfortable
with the steps. Then move on and add the next tool. You'll be amazed
by these ancient, natural techniques for happiness and inner peace.

Note

1. Giovanni Maciocia, *The Foundations of Chinese Medicine: A Compre-
    hensive Text for Acupuncturists and Herbalists* (Edinburgh: Churchill
    Livingstone, 1989), pp. 132–141.

Part One

THE TAO OF EMOTIONS

CHAPTER 1

THE VALUE OF EMOTIONS

WHY DO WE HAVE EMOTIONS IN THE FIRST PLACE? Many of us experience them as a disturbance, something out of our control. But they're not simply a thorn in our side. They are natural energy responses to what we experience through our senses. They're vital messages from our Soul, our higher self, to our personality or body.

Please note that many Western spiritual books use the terms *Soul* and *Spirit* as one and the same. However, in Taoism and some other esoteric writings, our Soul is the intermediary between our personality or body and our Spirit.

British spiritual teacher Ronald Beesley clarifies the distinction between Soul and Spirit. "The Spirit is of God [Tao]. Soul's one objective is to raise our consciousness to the level of Spirit. Soul is the active part of our being. It seeks out our fears and our inhibitions and makes us confront them. It supports us in facing and cleansing ourselves of these weaknesses. Our Soul is a loving parent and wise teacher."[1]

All emotions are the raw materials of human life, and they function as the guidance system for our decisions and actions. They are the raw materials for music, painting, drawing, sculpture, theater, film, dance, poetry, and fiction. Our emotions are spiritual treasures.

What are the messages of the positive emotions? The softer, yin emotions of calmness, gentleness, appreciation, kindness, and tenderness tell us we're in harmony with our higher selves, and so with Tao. The exciting, yang emotions of eagerness, enthusiasm, delight, happiness, ecstasy, and bliss tell us we're moving forward splendidly, also in harmony with Tao.

Negative Emotions: Catalysts for Growth

So, why do we have negative, painful emotions instead of just positive, pleasurable ones? Physical pain is a distress signal that some part of our body needs help. So, too, emotional pain is a distress signal that some aspect of our life needs help. The word *emotion* comes from the Latin word *emovere*, meaning to move out, move away. Despair, worry, fury, jealousy, and terror are marvelous teachers, motivating us with their sting to *move out, move away* and into harmony, joy, and courage.

The tragedy of modern life is that so many of us don't allow ourselves to feel the natural pain, and learn the lessons, of the turbulent emotions. We waste our precious time paralyzed by fear, denial, and repression. We self-medicate with food, alcohol, prescription and recreational drugs, electronic toys, entertainment, sex, overwork, and the media. Our bodies pay the price in discomfort, malfunction, and disease. Our minds pay the price in separation and alienation from our true selves. As Eckhart Tolle says: "Every addiction arises from an unconscious refusal to face and move through your own pain. . . . You are using something or somebody to cover up your pain."[2]

Reconnecting to Our True Feelings

If we are experiencing this alienation from our feelings, doing the Six Healing Sounds and Inner Smile daily will reconnect us to our internal organs; they, in turn, will restore our awareness of our true feelings. How long will this take? We can't give you a time frame, because each person is unique. However, most people feel calmer and more relaxed the first time they do these practices. Some people don't feel an obvious change for a few weeks or even a few months. But be assured, you will be changing your emotional and physical energy to a healthier state, even though the change may be subtle at first. Mantak Chia's forty-five years of practicing and teaching the Healing Sounds and Inner Smile, and Dena's twenty-six years, have convinced us of their benefit. Not one student has ever complained that they don't work. Those who use them as a daily tool always marvel at their healing power.

Facing, learning from, and transforming our negative feelings is an act of courage. It's a conscious choice that takes patience, self-honesty, forgiveness, and determination. It requires a commitment of time — to untie those emotions that have bound us up. Ultimately, we will save time, by having greater happiness, greater health, and a longer life. This demanding process is the crucible that transmutes negative energies into happiness and harmony. Our suffering is no longer a tragedy. It becomes the fuel that molds us into better human beings. It's a form of purification. And having endured and transcended emotional pain, we have more compassion for others who are still lost in turmoil. Chi kung (qigong) gives us many powerful and practical methods for igniting the fire beneath the crucible of transformation. The Six Healing Sounds and the Inner Smile are two of the most basic and important ones.

Notes

1. Ronald P. Beesley, *Esoteric Christianity* (Kent, England: White Lodge Publications, 1975), pp. 36–40. This is a close paraphrase of what Beesley says.
2. Eckhart Tolle, *The Power of Now: A Guide to Spiritual Enlightenment* (Novato, CA: New World Library, 1997), p. 127.

CHAPTER 2

TAO

A Natural, Gentle Way of Living

The Tao that can be told is not the eternal Tao.
The name that can be named is not the eternal name.

LAO TZU, *Tao Te Ching*[1]

YES, TAO IS BEYOND DEFINITION. However, it helps to have some idea of what it means. The Chinese word *Tao* literally means "way" or "path." Tao can be called the way of nature, the natural order of the universe. It may also be known as the Source of all that is, the ineffable, or God. It is infinite, eternal, and continually changing. The presence of Tao is within us and outside us. It is the unity of all beings and all things. It is the path of direct, divine experience. Unconditional love, harmony, and balance are its essence. Intuitive knowledge and spontaneous actions are its forms of expression. As the one force that governs the whole universe, Tao is not a religion, but it embraces all religions.

The Philosophy of Tao: Taoism

Tao will always be a mystery, greater than we can ever fathom. However, we can name, study, and practice the five-thousand-year-old

Chinese philosophy Taoism, which has had a profound influence on Chinese culture. Taoism seeks to align us with the sacred in our daily lives. Its basic focus is on how to live long, happy, healthy, productive lives that are in harmony with nature, of benefit to humankind, and conducive to spiritual growth. Its principles are presented in the twenty-five-hundred-year-old classic spiritual book *Tao Te Ching*, written by Lao Tzu, who lived in about the sixth century BCE.[2] This ancient treasure offers profound, succinct "poems" illustrating and inspiring wisdom in daily life. Written at a time of wars, materialism, and corrupt rulers, its lessons are especially relevant for our complex, turbulent society today.

Tao Te Ching is the most frequently translated book of all time. There are more than one hundred translations worldwide, and more than forty of these are in English. Lao Tzu's classic form of the Chinese language is enigmatic and evocative. One word can have many meanings and can be used as a noun, verb, or adjective, depending on the context. As a result, no single translation is the definitive one. We compared eight different translations of the book and chose selections from the three that we felt were clearest, were most relevant to our times, and which conveyed the poetic nature of the original.

A later Taoist philosopher, Chuang Tzu, who lived in about the fourth century BCE, supports and elaborates the ideas of *Tao Te Ching* in stories and parables. We've used references from *The Essential Chuang Tzu*, translated by Sam Hamill and J.P. Seaton.

The two practical branches of Taoism are chi kung — that is, meditations and physical exercises — and its offspring, Traditional Chinese Medicine (TCM), which includes acupuncture and herbology. Both chi kung and Chinese medicine work with refining, balancing, and raising a person's life-force energy for maximum health, happiness, creativity, longevity, and spirituality.

There is one small branch of Taoism that is an organized religion with rituals and hierarchy. However, at its core, Taoism is opposed to hierarchy and rigid structure. Our book does not deal with religious Taoism. Instead, it presents practical tools for self-healing painful emotions. Many practitioners of chi kung find it compatible with Christianity, Judaism, Buddhism, and Hinduism, as well as with agnosticism. Conversely, its celebration of individual experience, intuition, and freedom of expression make it incompatible with dogmatic religions or cults. In Taoism, no master or guru is set above others. Teachers are certainly respected, but everyone is equal before Tao. Universal Love is directly available to all.

The ancient Taoist masters were intuitive scientists of nature and of mystical states. They lived simply, patiently and carefully observing themselves, the animals, plants, and minerals, the moon, stars, and planets — and all without even a telescope. What they concluded was that there are definite patterns, rhythms, and cycles recurring in all forms of life: we humans are a microcosm of the macrocosm that is the universe. They discovered how to live in harmony with the patterns, rhythms, and cycles they observed, this natural order. They also created exercises and meditations to maximize their life-force energy by mimicking the movements or qualities of animals, trees, mountains, water, wind, and sun. And they chose to share their wisdom and knowledge with those who were receptive.

The intuitive, scientific investigations of Taoists created TCM, as well as the martial arts. Taoists also invented metal alloys, porcelain, dyes, the compass, and gunpowder.[3] They had a major influence on Chinese cuisine, classical painting, and poetry.

Some Taoist masters lived as hermits; some lived in the thick of Chinese society. In a few enlightened regimes, Taoists were given responsible positions in the government, where they taught and advised the rulers. Lao Tzu himself was head of the national library of the Zhou dynasty. In despotic regimes, Taoists were feared as rebels and were persecuted. Regardless, at all times, Taoists were noted for living very long, extraordinary lives, remaining healthy and productive through their advanced years. Even in today's complex, turbulent, and polluted world, chi kung practitioners reap the same benefits.

Basic Principles of Taoism

Let's consider some of the basic principles of Taoism. Being aware of them can deepen the effects of the *Emotional Wisdom* techniques.

Our Divine Origin

> *For it [Tao] can act as the mother of all things.*

> *For the Way gives them life;*
> *its power nourishes them,*
> *mothers and feeds them,*
> *completes and matures them,*
> *looks after them, protects them.*

> *Tao Te Ching*[4]

The ancient Taoists believed that all life originated from the Primordial Void, or Wu Chi in Chinese, also known as Tao. Something stirred within the Wu Chi, creating the positive and negative poles of yin and yang. The interactions of yin and yang created all universal processes and all matter. Western science calls the stirrings of Wu Chi that created life the big bang, the cosmic explosion that occurred 15 to 20 billion years ago.[5]

All beings are children of Tao, also called the Way. We all have a direct connection to Tao in our hearts: our Original Spirit, a spark of the divine, lives in our hearts. Original Spirit is our private line to the Source of all things. And it contains all the maternal qualities of Tao: unconditional love, devotion, patience, tenderness, gratitude, trust, generosity, intuition, and joy. These benevolent qualities match the position for the heart as perceived in Chinese medicine: it is the chief, or director, of the body. In other words, Tao, or the Divine, is not a separate, remote, superior being but is within our hearts, guiding, nourishing, protecting, and fulfilling us.

Life — Continual Self-Evolvement

So, if we all have a magnificent, powerful, loving heart, then why do we become aggravated, sad, or distressed? All these painful emotions are opportunities for growth, and they need to be addressed, to be learned from and transmuted. They are the result of being alienated from our Original Spirit and our Soul. In the process of becoming "civilized" and "mature," we learn to distrust, ignore, and harden our authentic selves and lose our childlike innocence and trust. We buy into society's promotion of materialism and the manipulation of others. We revere intellect, past knowledge, and authority more than our own intuitive wisdom. And in losing touch with our true selves, we lose a significant amount of our self-esteem. As author D. H. Lawrence recognizes, this alienation from our true divine nature is "the mistake" that makes us ill. He writes, "I am ill because of the wounds to the soul, to the deep emotional self.... Only time can help, ... and the freeing oneself from the endless repetition of the mistake which mankind at large has chosen to sanctify."[6]

A crucial goal of chi kung is to reopen the heart: to recognize and release the false idols of greed and egotism and reconnect to our

Original Spirit and our Soul. It's fascinating that the Chinese word *Shen* means "heart" or "mind" or "spirit." Chi kung and many Chinese medicine texts locate the mind and the Spirit in the heart. True Taoists follow their heart-minds when making decisions. The Six Healing Sounds, Inner Smile, and Releasing One Emotion practices are extremely helpful in our lifelong self-evolvement. They return us to our true essence and our self-esteem.

Chi = Energy, Internal and External

The unique genius of Taoism lies in its understanding and management of chi (pronounced *chee*), or energy. No other spiritual system is as clear, comprehensive, and sophisticated in its use and enhancement of chi. Chi is the activating energy of all movement in the universe; it is the life force of all formations, creatures, and things. In Japanese, it's called *ki*; in Sanskrit, it's *prana*; in Hebrew, it's *ruach*; in Tibetan, it's *lung*; in Lakota Sioux, it's *neyatoneyah*; in Arabic, it's *barraka*.[7]

The ancient Taoists recognized two main forms of chi that create and sustain life: internal and external.

Some in Western medicine call the energy inside us bioelectromagnetic energy. Ancient Taoists classified this internal chi into five subcategories: Hereditary or Original Chi, Life Force Chi, Sexual Chi, Internal Organ Chi, and Emotional Chi. In performing the Six Healing Sounds and Inner Smile, we improve all five forms of chi. We directly balance and increase our Emotional and Internal Organ Chi; this increases our Life Force Chi and our Sexual Chi, and enhances our Hereditary Chi. The ancient masters also mapped out the energy routes of the body that are identified as the meridians in acupuncture. The arm movements in the Six Healing Sounds activate the meridians connected to specific internal organs.

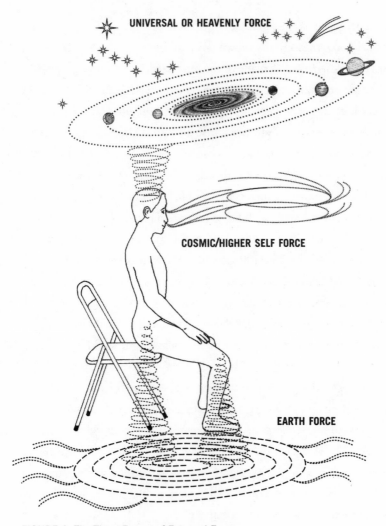

FIGURE 1: The Three Forces of External Energy

Tao masters divided the external energy — the energy that occurs outside the body — into three forces: the Universal or Heavenly Force, Cosmic or Higher-Self Force, and Earth Force. *Universal* or *Heavenly Force* includes the presence of Universal Love and the energies of all the galaxies of planets and stars. We receive Universal Force through the crown point at the top of our skulls. *Cosmic* or *Higher-Self Force* is made of the dust particles of stars and planets. It forms our human bodies. It's received through the third eye, the point between our eyebrows, and through the nose. *Earth Force* includes the energies of Mother Earth: all animals, plants, minerals, and natural formations (oceans, mountains, and so on) on the planet. We receive this energy directly through the soles of our feet and our sacrum. We receive it indirectly as well, by eating plants and animals that have predigested Earth Force for us. All three forces, Universal or Heavenly, Cosmic or Higher-Self, and Earth, are regarded as sacred, and are called the Three Pure Ones. They work together harmoniously to sustain all life-forms. Humans receive some of these three external energies directly, in a limited way; meditation allows us to increase our supply of external energy and store it in our bodies.[8] Chi kung teaches us how to store it safely, balancing it with Earth Force.

We lose much of our natural connection to these external forces when we hold on to negative emotions, eat a diet lacking sufficient nutrients, don't exercise regularly, deplete our Sexual Chi with excessive sexual intercourse, or are frequently exposed to environmental toxins. The Healing Sounds and Inner Smile can help to restore our connection to all three external forces — assuming we improve our emotions, our diet, and our environment, moderate our sexual activity, and exercise wisely and regularly.

The third force is a special concern in Taoism, in grounding our energy and connecting to Mother Earth. Most of us Westerners have a learned energy imbalance in our bodies; we live in our heads, ungrounded in our physical bodies and disconnected from the earth. The majority of our energy is concentrated in our heads and necks. We spend most of our time thinking with our brains, looking with our eyes (at computers, TV, films, video games), listening (to telephones, radios,

TVs, iPods), and speaking with our voices (in conversations face-to-face or by phone). We ignore our feelings and our bodies' messages of discomfort. This neglect shows first as stress or as aches and pains and mild dysfunctions; eventually, it develops into serious diseases.

Another energy imbalance results from spiritual methods that emphasize our connection to Universal or Heavenly Force (celestial energy), but which slight or negate our earth connection. This unbalanced focus can result in mild to severe energy blockages, manifesting as dizziness, spaciness, headaches, or "kundalini syndrome" (runaway energy) in the head or elsewhere. Unless they're reversed, these blockages can lead to physical or mental illness or to being accident-prone. Unfortunately, there are many spiritual seekers today who struggle with these difficulties.

Chi kung cures and prevents both headiness and runaway energy with five practices: Six Healing Sounds and the Inner Smile (which transform painful emotions), Microcosmic Orbit Meditation (which circulates and stores chi), and tai chi and Iron Shirt chi kung (which "root" our bodies to the earth). "Head in the clouds, feet on the ground" is the Taoist ideal for a spiritual practice and for being in the now, fully present in the body, in this moment of time, on this planet Earth.

Yin and Yang: Opposites Create Movement and Life

For being and non-being arise together;
hard and easy complete each other;
long and short shape each other;
high and low depend on each other.

Tao Te Ching [9]

A fundamental pattern recognized by the ancient Taoists is that every part of the universe is in constant motion, continually changing and transforming. Every organism is either contracting or expanding at any given point in time. In addition, energy can never be created or destroyed; it can only be changed.

FIGURE 2: Yin/Yang Symbol

This leads us to the next basic principle: the dynamic interplay of opposites creates all movement and life in the universe. All organisms have both yin and yang energies within them. The original, ancient meaning of yin is "the shady side of the hill," and the original meaning of yang is "the sunny side of the hill." Yin is the feminine aspect, and yang is the masculine. Yin is darkness, stillness, and contraction. Earth and water are yin. Yang is light, activity, and expansion. Heaven, sun, and fire are yang.

In our bodies, the front is yin and the back is yang. Each of our major internal organ systems functions as part of a pair of organs, with one yang and the other yin. Each yin/yang pair interacts with all the other pairs and contributes to balancing the whole body.

In our activities, yin is the feminine aspect of inner states: receptivity, quiet, acceptance, intuition, nurturing, planning, and integration. Yang is the masculine aspect of outer states: forward action, rational thought, assertiveness, competitiveness, and manifesting. Look at the tai chi symbol in the illustration: the black area represents yin; the white area represents yang. These two energies are interdependent and continually interacting with each other. Neither can exist without the other. Each has a seed of the other in its center and, if carried to an extreme, will change into its opposite.

The practical meaning of the yin/yang relationship is that we must always seek balance in our bodies, our minds, our emotions, and our activities. We must learn to balance our compact, quiet, inner processes with our expansive actions in the outer world. If we only stay at home, thinking and planning, we become insular and never act on our plans. If we only act and interact out in the world, we can't hear our inner wisdom or plan our actions carefully. We become too susceptible to other people's agendas and emotions and get burned out from so much activity. In the business sphere, if we expand our business too quickly and too much, it will falter and become small. Listening to the messages of our body and our emotions will help us maintain the balance between contracting and expanding.

Tai chi is a Taoist moving meditation that perfectly balances yin and yang. We begin and end the exercise at center. We alternate between moving out from the center of the body (yang) and returning to the center (yin). The movements are circular, slow, and continuously flowing. Although tai chi looks almost effortless (yin), it feels both powerful and relaxing (yang and yin balanced).

The Five Processes and Elements

Yin and yang interactions follow five different energy patterns: energy rising, energy gathering and sinking, energy expanding, energy solidifying, and energy stabilized. These processes operate and interact in all movement of energy — all life — in the universe.

Each of the Five Elements in nature incorporates one of these patterns. Note that Taoism configures the Elements somewhat uniquely: Fire, Water, Wood, Metal, and Earth. Fire is energy rising. Water is energy gathering and sinking. Wood is energy expanding. Metal is energy solidifying. Earth is energy stabilized.[10] When we work with the Six Healing Sounds, the Five Elements relate to particular emotions. For instance, depression is Metal energy, or solidifying energy. Fear is Water energy, or gathering and sinking energy.

The Creation Cycle and the Controlling Cycle

Each of the Five Processes and Elements interacts with and influences the others, according to particular sequences. The most important sequences are the Creation Cycle and the Controlling Cycle. The Creation Cycle expands energy; the Controlling Cycle contracts it. Together, they balance and check each other.

The Creation Cycle follows the order of the seasons: autumn, Metal; winter, Water; spring, Wood; summer, Fire; late summer, Earth. The Six Healing Sounds follow this order. Each of the Elements of the Creation Cycle creates or generates the next one. Thus, Metal creates Water; Water creates Wood; Wood creates Fire; Fire creates Earth; Earth creates Metal.

Each Element is also the child of the previous one. For example, Wood is the mother of Fire, and also the child of Water. The mother element nourishes its child element. We make use of this relationship later, when we suggest foods to alleviate specific negative emotions. If one organ and its Element in your body is weak, you can strengthen it with foods from both its mother and its child Elements.

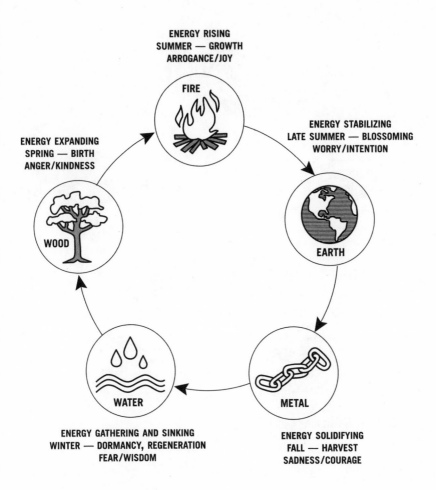

FIGURE 3: Creation Cycle

In the Controlling Cycle, each Element controls or checks the next Element and is controlled or checked by the previous one. Thus Wood controls or inhibits Earth and is controlled or inhibited by Metal.

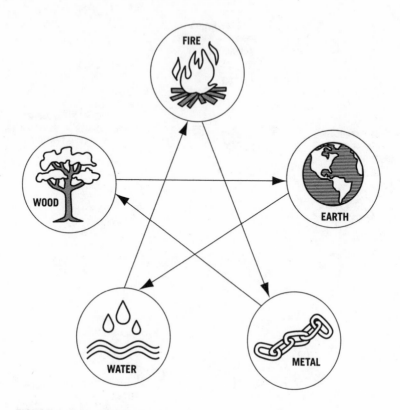

FIGURE 4: Controlling Cycle

Moderation

The balance of yin and yang is the golden mean, the wisdom to observe moderation in all areas of life. Extremes are exhausting and unhealthy. *Too much or too little* emotion, food, physical activity, mental activity, sexual expression, or socializing is harmful. Even too much joy, coming too suddenly, can be too much of a good thing. Our bodies know the importance of moderation. If we engage in too many activities in one day, we feel the need to slow down the next day. If we eat too much, we have little appetite for the next meal. The reverse is also true: very little activity, or a severely restricted diet, also distresses our bodies. The golden mean concept teaches us to take all triumphs and failures with a grain of salt. Since any circumstance in life could turn around in a second, it's best not to get deliriously happy or clinically depressed over the ups and downs we're likely to encounter. So-called misfortunes can turn out to be bridges to inner growth and great achievements. For example, illness can be the catalyst for healthy quantum leaps in our emotions, diet, and work life. Losing a job can motivate us to find a better job, to get new training and a more fulfilling occupation, or to start our own business.

Body Wisdom

Taoism teaches some unique wisdom about the body. All parts of our body interact and are interdependent. Therefore, an imbalance in one organ or part adversely affects the entire body. So chi kung practices and TCM work to strengthen the whole body, as well as to restore that ailing organ or part. Another important tenet is that the body has an amazing ability to heal and restore itself as long as we support this healing with the appropriate food, adequate rest, moderate exercise, elimination of toxins, moderate sexual relations, and positive emotions.

Chi kung practitioners are in tune with their bodies. They consciously develop awareness of their internal organs, which give them kinesthetic messages of harmony or imbalance. Most importantly, they've learned to use their hearts and abdomens as additional "brains"; these organs receive and express emotions — often more truthfully than the rational left brain in the head. And when we use these lower brains, the head brain can rest and rejuvenate itself.

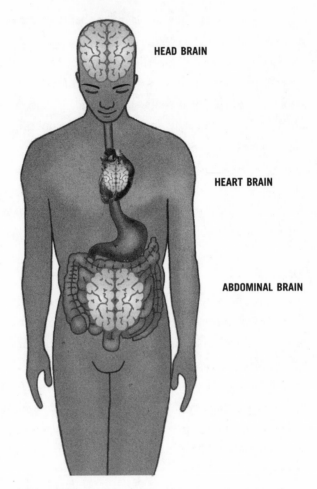

HEAD BRAIN

HEART BRAIN

ABDOMINAL BRAIN

FIGURE 5: Our Three Brains

Western science is beginning to acknowledge the existence of the abdominal brain. Dr. Michael D. Gershon, in his book *The Second Brain*, presents the results of studies that prove that the enteric nervous system (the esophagus, stomach, and large and small intestine) has a vast supply of nerve cells that receive and send messages and respond to emotions independently of our head brain. He notes too that the "gut brain" can be more accurate than the head brain in emotional responses.[11] So pay attention to your "gut responses."

Unlike some other spiritual systems that consider the body to be inferior, or even sinful, Taoism honors the body as the temple of the Spirit. The body has to be kept healthy and vital in order to have a fruitful, joyous life, and in order for us to live long enough to develop spiritually. All functions and needs of the body are regarded as holy; therefore, sex, coupled with love, is a spiritual act. When we take loving care of our body, our emotions, and our environment, we are attuned to receiving Universal or Heavenly Force. As Tao Huang has observed, "In its natural state, our body is in resonance with the universe and nature through the very crystalline structure of the bones, . . . as well as through its glands and organs."[12]

Notes

1. Gia-Fu Feng and Jane English, *Lao Tsu: Tao Te Ching* (New York: Vintage Books, 1972), chap. 1.

2. Wang Keping, *The Classic of the Dao: A New Investigation* (Beijing, China: Foreign Languages Press, 1998), i. The exact dates of Lao Tzu's birth and death are not known, but this recent scholarly book from China examines the evidence and concludes that he lived from 580 to 500 BCE.

3. Daniel Reid, *The Tao of Health, Sex, and Longevity* (London: Simon & Schuster, 1996), chap. 25, p. 34, chap. 51, p. 66.

4. Ursula K. Le Guin, *Lao Tzu: Tao Te Ching* (Boston: Shambhala, 1997), pp. 34, 66.

5. Mantak Chia and Maneewan Chia, *Awaken Healing Light of the Tao* (Rochester, VT: Inner Traditions, Bear & Co., 2008), pp. 15, 16.

6. D. H. Lawrence, *The Complete Poems of D. H. Lawrence*. Ed. Vivian de Sola Pinto and Warren Roberts (New York: Viking Press, 1971), p. 620.

7. Chia and Chia, *Awaken Healing Light of the Tao*, p. 34.

8. Ibid., pp. 19–23.

9. Le Guin, *Lao Tzu*, chap. 2, p. 4.

10. Chia and Chia, *Awaken Healing Light of the Tao*, pp. 17, 18.

11. Michael D. Gershon, *The Second Brain* (New York: HarperCollins, 1998), p. xiii.

12. Tao Huang quoted in Dennis Huntington, introduction to *Door to All Wonders*, by Mantak Chia and Tao Huang (Rochester, VT: Inner Traditions, Bear & Co., 2001), p. 13.

CHAPTER 3

THE SPIRIT OF TAO IN ACTION

Te

I have three treasures.
The first, mercy,
the second, moderation,
the third, modesty.

Tao Te Ching [1]

HOW DID LAO TZU'S FOLLOWERS REMAIN MERCIFUL, moderate, and modest despite the violence, inequities, and harsh laws of their time? They looked to his book *Tao Te Ching* for guidelines and inspiration. The original meaning of the word *Te* is "ascend, rise, and elevate." According to Mantak Chia and Tao Huang, the word *Te* means "kind action, virtue, beauty, and gracious behavior." [2] Other translators define it as power, strength, or integrity. Arthur Waley, a scholar of Chinese culture, defines *Te* as "latent power," an action that has "the potential for peace and prosperity." [3] Summing up all these interpretations, let's say that Te is benevolence in our daily actions — acting with integrity for the good of all beings.

This ancient wisdom has much to say to all of us today. Using *Tao Te Ching* and the writings of Chuang Tzu as our guides, and adding our own experiences as chi kung practitioners and teachers, we've summarized Te's guidelines for daily life. Consider it a model for your inspiration. None of us are already perfect; we're works in progress. As Mantak Chia is fond of saying, there is no sin, there is no hell; we're all working our way to our own heaven.

Kindness and Compassion

So wise souls are good at caring for people,
never turning their back on anyone.
Good people teach people who aren't good yet;
the less good are the makings of the good.

Tao Te Ching[4]

"Wise soul" is modern translator Ursula Le Guin's choice name for the ideal person continually referred to in *Tao Te Ching*. Other translators call this exemplary person "sage," "great man," "saint," or "wise man," and almost all use the pronoun *he*. We prefer Le Guin's "wise soul." It includes both genders, it includes those of us who are not acclaimed, and it fits with our book's title.

Let's start with a general description of wise souls. These are gentle, positive individualists who believe they create their own destiny by their alignment with Tao. Their humanity, calmness, and self-discipline give them an inner power that other people admire and emulate. This power is a magnet that draws to them what they need: loving relationships, meaningful work, and sufficient income. They live in harmony with nature, choosing their food and activities in accordance with its seasons and cycles. Taking their cue from Tao, the creator and nurturer, they treat everyone equally, with kindness and compassion. They avoid judging and blaming others.

Nonviolence

Violence and aggression destroy themselves.

Even the best weapon
is an unhappy tool,
hateful to living things.

To enjoy using weapons
is to enjoy killing people.
To enjoy killing people is
to lose your share in the common good.

Tao Te Ching [5]

Wise people shun violence and aggression, especially war. They defend themselves and their loved ones when necessary, but they never initiate violence. They walk away from potential conflict and don't care if they are called cowards. Love and kindness are the greatest powers in the universe. They are our ultimate protection and will guide us to avoid or transcend conflict.

Simplicity

The five colors
blind our eyes.
The five notes
deafen our ears.
The five flavors
dull our tastes.
Racing, chasing, hunting,

drives people crazy.
Trying to get rich
ties people in knots.
So the wise soul
watches with the inner
not the outer eye,
letting that go,
keeping this.

Tao Te Ching[6]

Simplicity is valued by wise souls. They choose to live simply, rather than waste their precious energy on obtaining, caring for, and protecting a great many things. They speak succinctly, saying only what is most important and knowing that less is more. They choose their activities carefully, avoiding unnecessary ones as well as excess stimulation.

Self-Knowledge and Self-Improvement

Knowing other people is intelligence,
knowing yourself is wisdom.
Overcoming others takes strength,
overcoming yourself takes greatness.

Tao Te Ching[7]

Wise ones are inner-directed. They take responsibility for their actions and the consequences that follow. They acknowledge and correct their weaknesses. More than outer achievement, they prize the daily cultivation of kind, compassionate, gracious actions — the expression of Te. Though they value and practice meditation and exercise, they know that Te is the highest expression of Tao.

Meditative Ability

So the sage's governing methods are:
Emptying the mind,
Vitalizing the stomach,
Softening the will,
Strengthening the character.

Tao Te Ching[8]

Through meditation, wise people have learned how to empty their minds, to clear away the extraneous, superficial, repetitive thoughts that disturb their peace and block their deepest perceptions. Freeing their minds of this chatter, they meditate to refine and increase their chi, their life-force energy; they center and store reserve chi in the navel area (vitalizing the stomach). Their chi softens their egos (the will), and this opens their connection to Original Spirit, Tao. They are then able to think, act, and speak according to their highest truth (strengthening the character).

Wise souls are aware of and sensitive to the flow of their life-force energy, always moving toward balance and harmony. They are also sensitive to the energies of those around them. Their positive, calm energy and their desire to help all beings enhance all their interactions with others.

Spontaneity and Intuition

Set your heart and mind on the One. . . .
Don't listen with your ear;
listen with your heart and mind.
Then, stop listening with your heart and mind
and listen with your ch'i,

the very energy of your body.
The ch'i is empty.

. . . .

It is able to attend upon all phenomena.

The Essential Chuang Tzu [9]

Spontaneity is the wise ones' gift of expression. Since they are attuned to their Original Spirits, and to Tao, they are able to respond naturally and uniquely to every person and situation. They are playful and have an innocent humor. They trust their intuitive wisdom over blindly accepting the theoretical knowledge of others or the opinions of "experts" or authority figures. Their spontaneity, flexibility, and concentration also make them especially creative in the fine arts, the healing arts, leadership, or any life challenges. They thrive by living in the now.

Forgiveness

Meet injury with the power of goodness.

Tao Te Ching [10]

Accepting and generous in their relationships, wise souls are aware of other people's natures and limitations and do not judge or condemn them. They teach indirectly, by their examples. If a person or situation remains negative, the wise ones forgive and walk away. Forgiveness is essential for our emotional health, our physical health, and our spiritual progress.

However, forgiveness does not mean allowing ourselves to be victimized by others — which is called "idiot compassion" in Buddhist writings. Victimization is a form of emotional violence that harms both the perpetrator and the recipient. The transformative power of goodness enables us to either change a victimizing situation or walk away.

Humility

And so the wise soul
predominates without dominating,
and leads without misleading.
And people don't get tired
of enjoying and praising
one who, not competing,
has in all the world
no competitor.

Tao Te Ching[11]

Wise souls are humble. They don't call attention to their skills and accomplishments. A job well done supplies an inner reward. In leadership positions, wise souls are pleased when their followers feel they have led themselves.

They're humble in another sense as well: they do not judge the behavior of others. Our human perception is always limited and subjective. Unless we walk in their sandals, we can't really know or understand all the reasons and meanings for other people's actions. It's enough to monitor our own behavior.

Wise souls are also humble in their respect for Tao. We humans are tiny sparks of the great divine Source. We cannot know or understand all of its vast mystery and power.

Appropriate Action

In the pursuit of learning, every day something is acquired.
In the pursuit of Tao, every day something is dropped.

Less and less is done
Until non-action is achieved.
When nothing is done, nothing is left undone.
The world is ruled by letting things take their course.
It cannot be ruled by interfering.

Tao Te Ching[12]

Lao Tzu's concept of nonaction can easily be misunderstood as passivity, or doing nothing. Chuang Tzu explains that nonaction means taking no rash or inappropriate action — no overreaction. Allow events to unfold according to their intrinsic nature. And then, if we are going with the flow of an event, we will automatically take the perfect action at the perfect time. As great performers, athletes, and artists do, we will find ourselves in the zone, surprising ourselves with our finesse. We'll be in the sweet spot, riding the face of the wave.

Integrity and Skill

It's easy to shatter delicate things,
easy to scatter little things.
Do things before they happen.
Get them straight before they get mixed up.
It's just as they've almost finished
that people go wrong.
Mind the end as the beginning.

Tao Te Ching[13]

Contrary to the misconception of nonaction, wise ones perform all tasks with efficiency and skill, looking after all the important details, especially at the beginning and the end of a project. Once they have chosen to do a project, no matter if it is small or large, they carry it out to the best of their ability. Anything worth doing is worth doing well. They also know that the positive completion of a project releases new, stronger energy for the next project.

Most likely, excellence in our work will lead to greater work opportunities. And excellence in our interpersonal relationships will bring us more love and more chi. But when we are engaged in a project, the best focus is to serve the needs of the project moment by moment. We focus with joy on the process, rather than worry about the reward. If we serve the *now* with devotion, we pave the way for a bountiful tomorrow.

Gentleness and Flexibility

A man is born gentle and weak.
At his death he is hard and stiff. . . .
Therefore the stiff and unbending is the disciple of death.
The gentle and yielding is the disciple of life.
Thus an army without flexibility never wins a battle.
A tree that is unbending is easily broken.
The hard and strong will fall.
The soft and weak will overcome.

Tao Te Ching [14]

Gentleness and flexibility are the hallmark of wise souls. Since they are securely grounded in their bodies and firmly aligned with compassion, wise souls are able to yield gracefully to opposition by people or events, or to change directions when necessary. They accept and work with whatever circumstances they are faced with, for the good of all concerned. They maintain a positive attitude in the midst of adversity, trusting that the outcome will be beneficial.

Detachment and Humor

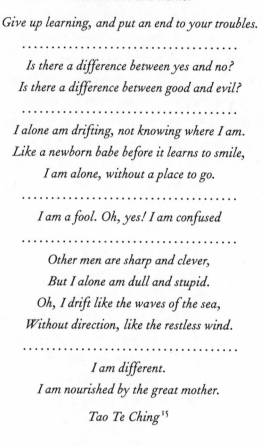

Give up learning, and put an end to your troubles.

. . . .

Is there a difference between yes and no?
Is there a difference between good and evil?

. . . .

I alone am drifting, not knowing where I am.
Like a newborn babe before it learns to smile,
I am alone, without a place to go.

. . . .

I am a fool. Oh, yes! I am confused

. . . .

Other men are sharp and clever,
But I alone am dull and stupid.
Oh, I drift like the waves of the sea,
Without direction, like the restless wind.

. . . .

I am different.
I am nourished by the great mother.

Tao Te Ching[15]

Living by what the scholars, the experts, or the moralists say will not nourish one's Soul or Spirit. Wise ones detach themselves from outer authority and family expectations and live by the guidance of Original Spirit, which communicates through the heart.

Often this means being adrift, living with uncertainty and ambiguity. After all, it takes time for the necessary components of a major life event to assemble, integrate, and emerge. As we drift, trusting we will find what we need, others will consider us dull witted, naive, weak, and foolish.

Humor is a marvelous form of detachment; we have to back off from a problem in order to laugh at it. Gentle, nonsarcastic humor lightens every interaction. It can even resolve a conflict amiably. And gently laughing at our own failings, our fears, and our blunders keeps us humble, balanced, and positive.

Daring to be different, we are nourished by the great mother.

Acceptance of Death

Peace: to accept what must be,
to know what endures.

. . . .

following the Tao,
the way that endures forever.
The body comes to its ending,
but there is nothing to fear.

Tao Te Ching[16]

Wise souls accept that death is inevitable. Since they are content and self-realized, they have no serious regrets when their lives end. They know that their kind, virtuous, gracious actions in life will live on in their loved ones and in all those whom they have helped. They perceive death as the natural end of one particular life — and the gateway to a higher state, a return to Tao.

Chuang Tzu was criticized for not mourning his wife's death appropriately. He did grieve for a while, but then he decided to celebrate her long and fruitful life and her transition to Tao, the mother of the world. He sang and played a drum at her funeral.

Notes

1. Ursula K. Le Guin, *Lao Tzu: Tao Te Ching* (Boston: Shambhala, 1997), chap. 67, p. 86.

2. Mantak Chia and Tao Huang, *Door to All Wonders* (Rochester, VT: Inner Traditions, Bear & Co., 2001), p. 170, p. xiii.

3. Arthur Waley, *The Way and Its Power: A Study of the Tao Te Ching and Its Place in Chinese Thought* (New York: Macmillan, 1956), pp. 31–32.

4. Le Guin, *Lao Tzu*, chap. 27, p. 37.

5. Ibid., chap. 42, p. 57; chap. 31, p. 42.

6. Ibid., chap. 12, p. 15.

7. Ibid., chap. 33, p. 44.

8. Chia and Huang, *Door to All Wonders*, trans. Huang with Edward Brennan, appendix 1, chap. 3, p. 243.

9. Chuang Tzu, *The Essential Chuang Tzu*. Trans. Sam Hamill and J. P. Seaton (Boston: Shambhala, 1998), chap. 4, p. 25.

10. Le Guin, *Lao Tzu*, chap. 63, p. 81.

11. Ibid., chap. 66, p. 84.

12. Gia-Fu Feng and Jane English, *Lao Tsu: Tao Te Ching* (New York: Vintage Books, 1972), chap. 48.

13. Le Guin, *Lao Tzu*, chap. 64, p. 82.

14. Feng and English, *Lao Tzu*, chap. 76.

15. Ibid., chap. 20.

16. Le Guin, *Lao Tzu*, chap. 16, pp. 22–23.

Part Two

EMOTIONS — MESSAGES
FROM OUR SOUL

CHAPTER 4

SADNESS AND DEPRESSION

A Modern Plague

PAINFUL EMOTIONS ARE MESSAGES FROM OUR SOUL telling us that we are out of balance, and that something needs attending to. In the next section of the book, we discuss how to transform these emotions by doing the Healing Sounds. But first, it's important to consider the messages of each of the "negative" emotions, as well as where they are housed in the body and foods that alleviate them.

The Valuable Messages of Sadness

What is our Soul saying when we feel sad, depressed, or lonely? Sadness is a natural response to a significant loss. The end of a marriage or close relationship can make us feel very sad. Certainly, the death of a parent, a child, a spouse, or a close friend can make us despondent. It's healthy to let ourselves deeply feel and express our sorrow. If we ignore, deny, or repress our grief, it will embed itself in our lungs or large intestine and cause them to malfunction. Eventually, we must let go of our sorrow, we must move beyond mourning, to acceptance. In the Taoist view, every challenge, every crisis, is an opportunity for us to learn — to grow wiser, kinder, and stronger.

Taoists view death as one's passing on to another state of energy, a transformation that returns us to our origin, Tao. Considering this viewpoint can help us accept the death of a dear one. Acceptance of our loss can lead to greater courage and a renewed sense of purpose. Since life is finite, we'd best concentrate on what is truly important to us.

The failure of a cherished project or business can also sadden us enormously, and the process of grieving for it is the same as for the loss of a person. We need to feel the sadness for a space of time and then let it go. Failure can be a powerful teacher. If we analyze the reasons for lack of success, and reverse the mistakes, then that failure may become the bridge to great success. A project may also fail because it's ahead of its time: society isn't ready for our particular innovation. For example, the opera *Porgy and Bess*, by George and Ira Gershwin and DuBose and Dorothy Heyward, is a masterpiece, but it was originally panned by New York critics and closed early with a large deficit. Van Gogh sold only a few paintings in his life — mostly to his brother. The key to transcending failure is to follow our heart's promptings. Original Spirit, Tao, communicates through our heart — and it is always true. It will guide us to the most beneficial actions.

If a beloved relationship or project is blocked or deteriorating, it's best to leave it alone for a while rather than falling into despair. Deepak Chopra offers good counsel in this regard: "...in order to acquire anything in the physical universe, you have to relinquish your attachment to it. You don't give up the intention and you don't give up the desire. You give up your attachment to the result."[1]

We can still keep our strong intention to repair said relationship or project, but we need to detach from *any immediate or specific results*. By backing off and trusting in our desire, the relationship or project is likely to blossom into unforeseen results far greater than we imagined. Individually, both Mantak Chia and Dena have experienced the wisdom of such detachment in major challenges.

Loneliness is a serious problem in modern society, and it can trigger depression. The high rate of divorce leaves many people without a spouse. Since men tend to remarry women younger than themselves, and since women live longer, loneliness is particularly common in older single women. Loneliness is compounded by the widespread phenomenon of adult children moving to other cities and states, far away from parents. Living in an apartment in a city, too, can engender loneliness. Most apartment dwellers are busy working and commuting and have limited time for socializing. Single people must make a concerted effort to find and maintain friendships. The Six Healing Sounds and the Inner Smile can release the pain of loneliness and create new energy and enthusiasm for friends and activities. Volunteering for charitable organizations that help people or animals in need or the environment is a great way to get a fresh, fulfilling perspective on life and to meet other giving people.

A significant number of Americans suffer from chronic depression without an obvious cause. We suggest that it's because they have depressed and repressed their natural, spontaneous selves. They have accepted the yoke of outer guidance and control by parents, teachers, and authority figures instead of cultivating and listening to their own unique inner wisdom. Their depression and repression probably relate to fear: fear of abandonment by a parent, fear of rejection by teachers or bosses, or fear of loneliness if they are considered to be "different."

Some gender differences may occur in chronic depression. Although social roles are changing somewhat, many women have been taught to be compliant and enabling with their fathers, brothers, husbands, and male children at the expense of their own feelings and desires. Many men have been taught they must always lead and "win" in their interactions with women and other men; this winning, too, is at the expense of their feelings and desires. Clearly, women must balance their yin internal processes with more yang external actions. And men need to balance their yang external actions with more yin internal processes. Happily, the women's rights movement in the last forty or so years has inspired many parents to raise their girls and boys to be equal and better balanced.

Sadness and Depression — Housed in Our Lungs and Large Intestine

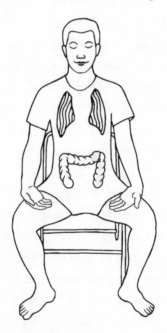

FIGURE 6: Lungs and Large Intestine

The lungs and large intestine house the emotions of sadness and depression. On the positive side, they house courage and the psychological qualities of letting go and of right action — taking the appropriate action at the appropriate time. Prolonged sadness and depression build up in these organs and weaken their positive attributes.

Western medicine informs us that the lungs and large intestine have crucial functions. All the cells of our body require a continuous and abundant supply of oxygen in order to function. Even a few minutes without oxygen can result in death. The lungs, nose, throat, trachea (windpipe), chest muscles, and diaphragm constitute the respiratory system; their job is to supply oxygen to the blood cells in the lungs and remove the waste by-product of metabolism, carbon dioxide. Most of our breathing is automatically controlled by the brain. When the body needs to get more oxygen and release carbon dioxide, the chest muscles and diaphragm expand, enlarging the chest cavity. The lungs expand, which creates negative air pressure; to equalize the pressure, air rushes into the lungs through the nose, mouth, and throat. Inside the lungs, blood cells absorb oxygen from the air and simultaneously release carbon dioxide. Then the chest muscles and diaphragm relax, contracting the lungs and forcing the air out through the throat, mouth, and nose. The oxygen-enriched blood cells continue on their journey, delivering oxygen to cells throughout the entire body in exchange for carbon dioxide.

The large intestine receives the waste food materials once digestion and absorption have occurred in the stomach and small intestine. Most of the water and salts in this waste are absorbed through its walls, and they enter the bloodstream. The large intestine excretes the remaining water and solid waste into the rectum, which eliminates it through the anus. In addition, friendly bacteria in the large intestine aid in producing vitamin K and some of the B vitamins.

In chi kung and Traditional Chinese Medicine, the lungs are seen as governing chi and respiration. They receive food chi from the spleen and combine it with inhaled air to form gathering chi; they spread this chi throughout the body. The lungs also receive body fluids from the spleen, change them to a fine mist, and spray them throughout the body, in the spaces between the muscles and the skin. They direct fluids down to the kidneys and bladder. They also spread Defensive or Protective chi throughout the body, also beneath the skin. The lungs influence the skin, the nose, the throat, the vocal cords, and the body hair. Because they control the inhalation of air and influence the skin, the lungs are the most external of the yin organs; they are the connection between the body and the environment. As a result, they are the organ most easily affected by extremes of wind, heat, cold, dampness, and dryness. Spiritually, the lungs house the Po, the Corporeal Soul, which returns to the earth when we die. (The Ethereal Soul, Hun, in the liver, returns with our Spirit to Tao.)

As noted in chapter 2, our organs are paired with other organs. The lungs are the yin organs paired with the yang large intestine. The large intestine receives waste and water from the small intestine; it absorbs some of the water and excretes the rest.

According to TCM and chi kung, each of the internal organ pairs is related to, and influenced by, a specific Element in nature. The lungs and large intestine are classified as related to the Element of Metal. The energetic nature of Metal is energy solidifying. If we have an excess of Metal energy, in the form of chronic sadness or depression, this means we have "solidified" and are clinging to past hurts or losses. We may collect material objects to compensate for those hurts or losses, becoming pack rats, unconsciously accumulating things to replace what we lost.

Physically, too much sadness (Metal: energy solidifying) can manifest in the lungs as frequent colds or flu, skin problems, asthma, emphysema, or lung cancer. In the large intestine, excess grief can turn into constipation or colorectal cancer. A vast number of Americans suffer from chronic constipation.

Diseases of the lungs and large intestine are among the major causes of death in the United States. Lung disease is the second leading cause of death; colorectal cancer is the third.

Learning from and transforming grief increases our courage and our ability to let go of past grievances. It gives us the energy and intuition necessary to take the most effective and appropriate action when it's needed.

Specific Foods and Color to Alleviate Sadness

TCM and chi kung view nutritious food and excellent digestion as crucial to optimal health. In fact, Chinese doctors have traditionally regarded food as the first line of defense when treating a disease, before herbs and medicines. Food is classified according to five specific tastes or flavors: spicy, salty, sour, bitter, and sweet. Each of these benefits a particular pair of internal organs. Five specific colors also enhance each pair of organs: white, blue or black, green, red, and yellow. This ancient belief is validated by modern science. Each of the colored pigments of our food has one or more antioxidants.[2] The healthiest diet includes all five tastes and all five colors. We can maximize the effectiveness of the Six Healing Sounds and Inner Smile in transforming negative emotions by eating particular foods and wearing specific colors.

Consider the following general suggestions about food. A healthy, balanced diet will energize and fortify your entire body. Eat as much fresh, locally grown, organic food as possible; avoid the toxic pesticides and fertilizers found in nonorganic food.

Avoid genetically modified food. We don't know the long-term effects of adding artificial genes to our body. The cellular biologist Dr. Bruce Lipton points to a study showing that "artificially created genes transfer into and alter the character of the beneficial bacteria in the intestines."[3] Our intestines are a major part of our immune system. We in the United States have already seen a significant increase in the incidences of cancer, diabetes, and obesity; meddling with Mother Nature in such a basic way as genetic modification may escalate these and other diseases. Unfortunately in the United States, with the exception of organic food, *almost all food is now genetically modified*. The major pharmaceutical companies control the distribution of seeds sold to most farmers, and these seeds are genetically modified. Avoid canned, processed, or irradiated food, even if organic; it has little or no nutritive value and, as a result, taxes your digestion, robs you of nutrients, contributes to excess weight, and lowers your immunity to disease.

Include lots of green vegetables in your diet to keep your blood on the alkaline side. Eliminate or greatly reduce foods with cane sugar; it makes your normally alkaline blood acidic, which reduces your immunity. (Notice how many people get colds or flu after bingeing on sweets at Christmas, Chanukah, or New Year's celebrations.) For sweeteners, substitute a small amount of organic raw honey or organic 100 percent pure maple syrup. Eat slowly, take small bites, and chew each one thoroughly until it is liquefied. Mix your food, even your juices, with lots of saliva; digestion begins in the mouth, with the saliva. Hastily chewed food results in indigestion, gas, bloating, constipation, or diarrhea and, worst of all, in poor nutrition for your body.

Every day, eat a variety of colors and all of the five tastes. We discuss each of these in detail later, with the emotion they relate to. To reduce sadness and strengthen your lungs and large intestine, include a *small* amount of spicy foods, such as those seasoned with curry, dill, garlic, ginger, hot peppers, onions, oregano, parsley, cayenne pepper, peppermint, or spearmint. Grow or buy fresh organic herbs; their flavors and nutrition are far superior to dried, packaged ones. You can also dry the extra herbs yourself and put them into jars. *However, if your lungs or large intestine are very weak, avoid spicy foods, which are the Metal Element. Instead, emphasize sweet foods, which are the Earth Element, and salty foods, which are the Water Element.* The mother of Metal, Earth, and the child of Metal, Water, will strengthen Metal. (See the index for page numbers of sweet and salty foods. Also see Creation Cycle, for an explanation of the mother and child relationship between the organs and their Elements.) When you have strengthened these organs with the Healing Sounds and Inner Smile, you may be able to gradually reintroduce spicy food to your diet.

Fall is the season when our lungs and large intestine are working the hardest. Fruits that ripen primarily in fall, such as grapes, persimmons, apples, and pears, are excellent for these organs. Broccoli, kale, parsley, pumpkin, turnip, watercress, and winter squash protect the mucous membranes of these organs.[4] White-colored foods contain isothiocyanates, which support the immune system, which is part of the lung–large intestine system.[5] So include cauliflower, turnip, parsnip, and daikon radish in your fall menus. Promote regular elimination by eating these raw foods: carrots, celery, radishes, apples, bananas, and pears. Boost your digestive enzymes dramatically by eating a few tablespoons of organic raw, unpasteurized sauerkraut, and drink some of the brine.

Periodically, do a mild colon cleanse with white or black fungus. You can purchase these at a Chinese herb store or online. Black fungus is an ingredient in mu shu, offered at many Chinese restaurants. White fungus has a curly texture and a neutral taste. Cook the fungus in water until it reaches a chewable consistency. Then eat a small amount with cereal, cooked vegetables, or scrambled eggs. The fungus becomes gelatinous in the colon and gently pulls out stubborn waste.

Wearing white clothes nourishes our lungs and large intestine. White clothing also highlights and complements our complexion. Don't restrict yourself to wearing white only in summer.

Because Metal is the element associated with these internal organs, take the time to appreciate the utility and strength of cars, other machines, tools, instruments, and tableware. Enjoy the beauty and radiance of metal sculpture and jewelry.

Notes

1. Deepak Chopra, *The Seven Spiritual Laws of Success* (Novato, CA: Amber-Allen Publishing and New World Library, 1993), p. 83.
2. Maoshing Ni, *Secrets of Self-Healing* (New York: Avery, 2008), p. 77.
3. Bruce Lipton, *The Biology of Belief* (Santa Rosa, CA: Mountain of Life Elite Books, 2005), p. 45.
4. Paul Pitchford, *Healing with Whole Foods: Oriental Traditions and Modern Nutrition* (Berkeley, CA: North Atlantic Books), pp. 312–33.
5. Ni, *Secrets of Self-Healing*, p. 77.

CHAPTER 5

FEAR AND NERVOUSNESS

Our Enemies and Friends

FEAR AND NERVOUSNESS ARE NATURAL RESPONSES to physical or emotional danger. A *little* fear or nervousness can help us enormously by giving us the extra adrenaline we need for a challenge. When we're facing a real danger, it gives us more energy to run away. When we're interviewing for a job or a special opportunity, mild fear energizes us to do our best. When we're speaking or performing publicly, a little fear can spark a newfound eloquence in us. Singer and songwriter Holly Near shared this thought with the audience at a concert Dena once attended: "I like to turn fear into fascination — or fun! — to figure out what I can learn from my fear."

The Valuable Messages of Fear and Nervousness

Let's distinguish between caution and fear. Caution is a healthy instinct: it warns us to be careful in a potentially dangerous situation.

It's wise to be cautious when we're crossing a busy intersection, when we're building a fire, or when we're driving on the freeway.

Excessive fear or nervousness is self-defeating. It paralyzes us; it keeps us from acting on our deepest desires. Fear is the opposite of love. Fear is the yin contraction opposing the yang expansion of love. Fear makes us smaller, heavier, drier, more rigid, and restricted. Fear blocks everything in our life: our body, our thinking, our actions, our spiritual progress. Even a small amount of love makes us larger, lighter, more flexible, more creative, more daring. A deep love for another person, an animal, or nature, or for a creative expression such as music, art, athletics, or gardening has a profound effect. This love releases the blockages and allows fresh energy to enter and renew us on all levels.

Many spiritual teachers have said that there are only two major emotions, love and fear. What about hate, anger, worry, sadness, and arrogance? These, they say, are all the offspring of fear. Fear is a lack of confidence in our future, a mind-set that convinces us that dire consequences are just around the corner, consequences we can't avoid or control. But feeling helpless is so painful that we push it away. We convert our fear into anger or hate against the perceived "enemy." Or we adopt an arrogant attitude to hide our fear. Or we channel the fear into excessive worry or depression. Or we become reckless daredevils who scoff at fear.

Society imposes some common gender imbalances concerning fear. It's more acceptable for females to express their fear, but less acceptable for them to express anger. The opposite is true for males: anger is more acceptable, and fear is a sign of weakness. Clearly, both genders can benefit from balancing emotions.

Unfortunately, we live in a society largely ruled by fear. Many of us have been raised with large doses of it. We can still hear echoes of our parents' teachings: "No! Don't do that! Don't take chances! You'll get hurt! You'll get punished!" The media reinforce our fears by focusing on calamities, murders and other crimes, and wars. Some political leaders do their part by convincing us that this is a dangerous, treacherous world, and that they'll protect us if we subscribe to their policies.

Fear and Nervousness — Housed in Our Kidneys and Bladder

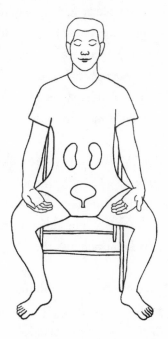

FIGURE 7: Kidneys and Bladder

Chi kung and Traditional Chinese Medicine recognize that fear is stored in the kidneys and bladder. Many of our students, and some of our instructors, are acupuncturists, and they all agree: kidney weakness is the norm in our society. No wonder.

The kidneys and bladder also house the positive emotions of gentleness and calmness, as well as the psychological traits of willpower and wisdom. A buildup of unresolved fear or nervousness weakens these desirable qualities.

The functions of the kidneys are essential to life. Allopathic (Western) medicine tells us that they filter our blood and excrete the waste materials as urine. They aid in maintaining the crucial balance of water, salts, and other substances in our blood. The kidneys also regulate the acid-alkaline balance in our body fluids, and they produce hormones to regulate our blood pressure and oxygen level and to stimulate the production of red blood cells.

The kidneys send waste material, as urine, down the ureters, the tubes, to the bladder. The bladder stores the urine and then releases it through the urethra. The functions of these organs are absolutely crucial to life.

In chi kung and TCM, the kidneys are called the Root of Life, because they store the body's Essence. Essence is the source of reproduction, development, and maturation. It is also the underlying material of all the organs of the body. The kidneys are yin and the bladder is yang. Spiritually, the kidneys house the Willpower Spirit, or Zhi in Chinese.

Water is the Element associated with the kidneys and bladder. The energetic nature of water is energy gathering and sinking. Chronic fear stresses our kidneys and bladder. This makes our water energy sluggish and stagnant. Our kidneys become impaired, less able to gather waste material from the blood, convert it to urine, and sink the urine down to the bladder to be released.

In TCM, the kidneys are seen as controlling our sex drive, hearing, bones, teeth, head hair, lower back, knees, ankles, and feet. Their associated glands are the sexual glands and the adrenal glands. So, living in fear may result in one or more of these problems: weak sexual energy, infertility, urinary problems, bladder infections, adrenal exhaustion, teeth and bone deterioration, hair loss, and knee, ankle, or foot problems. The picture is even worse when we consider the Taoist view that all the organs and systems depend on the kidneys for Essence, for vitality. Excessive fear eventually weakens all our internal organs and shortens our lives.

American society has an anxious, schizophrenic relationship to sex. Most popular songs are about seeking, finding, or losing a lover. Most films, plays, and TV shows routinely include sexual relationships in their plots. Many people long for healthy sexual relationships, and yet they also fear them. We are still influenced by the puritanical bias of the early European settlers, who saw sex as something shameful, something to feel guilty about. The sexual freedom of the 1960s has been restrained by fear of AIDS or other sexually transmitted diseases. The pornography industry earns billions by portraying sex as something forbidden and exploitative — a power to hold over others. Advertising uses attractive men and women in seductive poses to sell everything from cars to carpets.

Chi kung celebrates sex as a natural part of a loving, equal relationship. Both partners seek to please and pleasure each other as an expression of unconditional love. Clearing and transforming our painful emotions with the Healing Sounds and Inner Smile enhances both lovemaking and health by energizing the kidneys, bladder, and sexual organs, as well as all the other internal organs. Chi kung also has specific methods to enhance lovemaking and increase longevity. Sex becomes a form of rejuvenation and a spiritual catalyst. These methods are covered in Mantak Chia's books on Taoist sexual practices, listed under "Taoist Sexology" in the Selected References section near the end of the book.

Fear can be our worst enemy and our greatest friend. If ignored and denied, it robs us of the richness of life. If acknowledged and transformed, it leads us into balance and inner peace. The Six Healing Sounds and Inner Smile are potent energetic medicine for our poor depleted kidneys and bladder.

Most important, we can't allow fear to rule our lives. Regardless of the chaos and suffering we see around us, we must generate a positive nature every day. We can help others in need as we cultivate gentleness, willpower, and wisdom within ourselves. We can be a beacon of inner peace shining out to all we meet.

Specific Foods and Colors to Alleviate Fear

As we noted before, it's important to eat fresh, locally grown, organic food as much as possible. Avoid canned, packaged, irradiated, or genetically modified food. Avoid cane sugar; substitute a small amount of organic raw honey or 100 percent pure maple syrup. Eat all five tastes every day. Eat a variety of food colors every day, especially raw or lightly cooked greens. Include one or more raw, fermented foods daily; these are covered in the next chapter.

Winter is the season when our kidneys and bladder work the hardest. Support them in winter, and all seasons, by eating blue and black foods. These contain anthocyanins, which support the hormone system, which is part of the kidney and bladder system.[1] So include black beans, blueberries, blackberries, black olives, and dried seaweeds such as nori, kombu, kelp, and dulse. Seaweeds are an excellent source of minerals. Instead of eating potato chips, try snacking on dried dulse or nori; they're deliciously salty. Add them to your salads as well. Seaweeds are especially welcome in winter, since they are both black and salty. Salty is the taste that supports kidneys and bladder. Eat *very small amounts* of sea salt, preferably Celtic, which may require a salt grinder, or other quality organic sea salt. They're not only healthier but also their taste is outstanding. Use very small amounts of organic miso or tamari sauce (a higher grade of soy sauce). Other salty foods to include are organic free-range eggs; raw, aged goat cheese, especially salted feta; raw butter; and high-quality saltwater fish.

Note that many people who are lactose intolerant can digest and thrive on organic raw milk products. It's the pasteurization (heating) and homogenization (crushing) of most dairy products that probably cause the intolerance. If you can get raw organic butter, it's very beneficial; it's an excellent source of vitamins A, D, K, and E.[2] If you're a vegetarian, raw butter and egg yolks are your only source of animal fat. If raw organic butter is not available in your health food store, you may be able to get it and other raw dairy products from a local farmer. Ask the vendors at your local farmers' market for a contact, or go online. Margarine and other butter substitutes are loaded with toxic chemicals.

However, if your kidneys or bladder are very weak, it's best to minimize salty foods and to emphasize spicy and sour foods instead.

Wearing blue or black clothes enhances our kidneys and bladder and, as a result, helps to reduce fear. Black also balances our mental activities with its grounding effect. Ignore black's negative reputation; black clothes are elegant, authoritative, attractive . . . and slimming!

Water is the element associated with the kidneys and bladder. Our body is about 70 percent water, and we must continually replenish it with clean, filtered water. High-quality home water filters are superior to bottled water, which varies in its purity. Some brands are no better than tap water. Wash your fruits and vegetables with filtered water, and cook with it.

Daily Water Requirement

How much water should we drink each day? Many modern health professionals advise us to drink at least eight cups of plain water a day, in addition to any other fluids. TCM advises us to daily consume no more than six cups of all fluids combined, including those in fruits and vegetables, because it says this is how much the kidneys can comfortably filter in one day. Any more than six cups leads to water retention.

Naturopathic medicine, however, advises us to drink filtered water, half the amount in ounces of our body weight. Thus, if one weighs 140 pounds, he or she should drink seventy ounces, or about eight and a half cups. Acupuncturist Mikio Sankey agrees with this, because he believes that our modern society stresses our bodies with so many toxins in our food, our water, and our air, and with electromagnetic radiation from cell phones, microwaves, computers, and so on, that we need to drink more pure water to flush out these toxins. Freshly pressed organic vegetable juices also count as beneficial fluids, if drunk within fifteen minutes of making them. Soft drinks and bottled juices are not beneficial, because they are loaded with sugar and preservatives.[3]

Mantak Chia suggests these guidelines. If your urine is light yellow, this indicates you are consuming enough liquids. If your urine is dark yellow, you need more liquids in order for your liver to detoxify waste substances. Emptying the bladder five or six times a day is another indication that you are consuming the right amount of fluids.

Many health experts say it's best not to drink liquids with your meals, because water dilutes the hydrochloric acid and enzymes in the digestive system. However, Dena suggests that drinking a half cup of lukewarm filtered water with a few squeezes of fresh lemon about twenty minutes before a meal can improve your digestion.

So consider these differing recommendations, try the ones that call to you, and then let your own body wisdom be the final expert.

Be grateful for the gift of water to sustain life. Appreciate our oceans, lakes, and rivers; whenever possible, gaze at them and give thanks for their beauty, the food they supply to us, their transportation functions, and their recreational delights.

In the *Tao Te Ching*, Lao Tzu frequently equates Tao with water. Water flows from above and sinks into the earth. It is soft and yielding, but it can overcome fire, wood, earth, and stone. Sankey calls the kidneys "the sparkplugs that ignite the other systems."[4] Strengthening our sparkplugs by releasing fear will ignite our willpower and our wisdom, our gentleness and calmness.

Notes

1. Sally Fallon, with Mary G. Enig, *Nourishing Traditions*, 2nd ed. (Washington, DC: New Trends Publishing, 2001), p. 15.

2. Maoshing Ni, *Secrets of Self-Healing* (New York: Avery, 2008), p. 77.

3. Mikio Sankey, *Support the Mountain: Nutrition for Expanded Consciousness* (Inglewood, CA: Mountain Castle Publishing, 2008), pp. 140–141.

4. Mikio Sankey, *Discern the Whisper: Esoteric Acupuncture*, vol. 2 (Inglewood, CA: Mountain Castle Publishing, 2002), p. 53.

CHAPTER 6

ANGER

Nightmare and Catalyst

ANGER IS THE EMOTION that most people have trouble expressing appropriately and effectively. Chi kung and TCM include in the category of anger these variations: resentment, rage, jealousy, frustration, and stress. The psychological qualities of stubbornness and overcriticalness are closely related.

The Valuable Messages of Anger and Its Variations

Anger is a natural response to an interaction or situation that is not desirable for us or those we care about. It can also be a natural response to injustice toward other individuals or groups in the larger world. If we are attuned to our bodies, anger will bring on a strong sense of uneasiness or discomfort. We'll feel unbalanced until we express our anger, change the circumstances that caused it, or forgive the person or persons who sparked it.

Unfortunately, many people are not in touch with their anger or their bodies' signals. They've been taught that showing anger is harmful and wrong. They're ashamed of it, and they're afraid of it. So they ignore, deny, or repress their anger. As we've said before, it doesn't go away; it just goes underground and disturbs our physical and emotional well-being.

On the other hand, expressing anger or rage by verbally or physically attacking an opponent usually makes everything worse: it escalates the level of antagonism for both parties. A nasty verbal attack can ruin a relationship for good. A violent physical attack can lead to serious injury or even death.

Healthy Ways to Deal with Anger and Its Variations

First of all, we have to allow ourselves to feel our anger. If this is a problem for you, make a conscious choice to change this. Tell yourself you can learn how to feel anger without harming yourself or others. Do all the Healing Sounds exercises, which are covered in the next section of the book, once or twice a day. As you do the anger sequence, repeat the anger sound twelve or more times. Do the Inner Smile exercise once or twice a day. Do the Releasing One Emotion exercise a few times a week.

When you are able to feel your anger, you may find yourself expressing it more often and more vehemently than is necessary or effective. Don't panic! This is a sign of progress, to be able to express it at all. So work next on expressing it in a compassionate way — for the good of all concerned. As Lao Tzu says, "Meet injury with the power of goodness."[1] This is an art that we can develop and hone. It means stating our needs calmly, without putting the other person or persons down. Injecting goodwill into a tense situation can suddenly change it and produce a win-win outcome.

Here's an example of expressing mild or occasional anger in this way. Let's say your life partner has ignored your birthday, which upsets you. In a calm voice, tell him or her that you are angry, and give the reason for your anger. Use "I" language. For example: "When you ignore my birthday, I feel angry and hurt. I always buy you a present for your birthday and take you out to dinner. It's important to me that you celebrate my birthday." Now express goodwill and caring: "I really love you, and I want us to be closer and happier together."

If a calm, face-to-face expression of anger causes the other party to get defensive or furious, try writing a letter to him or her. Again, calmly give the reason for your anger, use "I" language, and sincerely express your desire to mend the relationship.

If neither approach will work, or if the situation will not permit any confrontation at all, write the letter anyway. Then read it aloud to yourself, with feeling, and burn it. On a higher level, the other party will receive your message and may even amend his or her behavior. At the very least, you'll feel better for having expressed your anger.

Keep in mind, too, that there are undesirable relationships and jobs that we are simply unable to improve despite our best efforts. The only way to release our anger is to leave, with goodwill and forgiveness.

Chronic rage is a deep-seated emotional problem that requires professional help to reverse. Often it's connected to emotional or physical abuse by an enraged parent, who may have been addicted to alcohol or drugs. A skilled therapist, counselor, or spiritual advisor can work in depth with one who is experiencing this problem, helping him or her understand and release rage.

Jealousy is a troubling emotion in the anger category. If we lack something in a meaningful area of life, it's easy to be jealous of people who have an abundance in this area. But rather than resent their good fortune, we can let their example inspire us. If you feel jealous of others, find out or analyze what they did to attract a loving life partner, a fulfilling job, a generous income, or whatever else you covet. Consciously look for clues and hints that will bring you what you desire. Focusing on jealousy will block your good fortune. Instead, imagine and feel the joy of having your wish already fulfilled. Create the positive energy that will attract what you desire.

Keep in mind that timing is a crucial factor in the events of our lives. It's possible that a particular desire remains unfulfilled because we are not ready to handle it with harmony and balance. For example, it's been said that many people who win the lottery squander their money and lose it.

Every relationship or possession requires time and attention if it is to flourish. So be sure you have made a space in your life for a life partner, a new job, a larger house, or whatever else you seek.

Be aware, though, that having excess material goods can drain your chi energy and your time. Everything you own — whether clothes, household goods, electronic devices, or cars — has to be maintained and repaired. In the nineteenth century, a much simpler time, William Wordsworth observed, "The world is too much with us. Getting and spending, we lay waste our powers. Little we see in nature that is ours." How true this is for our complex electronic age!

Suspicious jealousy of a spouse or romantic partner, not trusting him or her to be faithful, is also a deep-seated problem that calls for expert therapy, counseling, or spiritual guidance to reverse. It can be related to a childhood fear of abandonment by a neglectful or absent parent.

Forgiveness Is Crucial

Good people teach people who aren't good yet.
The less good are the makings of the good.

Tao Te Ching[2]

In order to fully heal our anger, we must forgive all parties involved, including ourselves. This is not an easy task, but it's crucial for our peace of mind. Consider that none of us are perfect, including those of us who are cleaning up our emotional baggage. We may be more evolved than certain others, but there are plenty of people who are ahead of us. Those whom we feel have hurt us may be younger Souls than we are. Most likely, we ourselves have made similar (or worse) mistakes earlier in our lives.

Our forgiveness is a powerful lesson for our adversaries. It can change an enemy into an admirer. We must also forgive ourselves for any part we may have played in a conflict. On a purely selfish level, we need to forgive in order to release the toxic anger that harms our health and inner peace.

Anger and Its Variations — Housed in Our Liver and Gallbladder

The positive emotions of kindness and generosity make their home in the liver and gallbladder. The psychological qualities of decisiveness, planning, and precision also dwell there. The negative emotions of anger, resentment, rage, jealousy, frustration, and stress, too, lodge in these organs, along with the traits of stubbornness, procrastination, and overcriticalness. The negatives diminish the positives.

The liver is an extremely complex and valuable organ. According to Western medicine, it's the chemical factory of the body. Its

FIGURE 8: Liver and Gallbladder

major functions include, among others, storing, regulating, and releasing glucose (blood sugar) into the bloodstream; forming blood plasma proteins; making bile, which splits fat particles into digestible size; detoxifying and eliminating harmful substances from our blood; and making a substance that prevents blood clotting.

The gallbladder is a muscular sac below the liver that stores the bile and releases it into the small intestine when needed for digesting fats.

In TCM, the liver is called "the general" and "the harmonizer" of the body. Rather than use militaristic terminology and assume that the body is a battlefield, let's call it the chief executive officer. According to Giovanni Maciocia, "It ensures the smooth flow of chi throughout the body, in all organs, and in all directions."[3] The liver also stores the blood and regulates the volume of blood according to the area and level of activity needed. It controls the tendons and ligaments that move the joints, nourishes and moistens the eyes and the nails,[4] and functions as the yin partner to the yang gallbladder. Spiritually, the liver houses the Ethereal Soul, or Hun in Chinese; this is the eternal part of our Soul, which leaves our body, with our Spirit, at death and returns to the Primordial Void — in other words, to our Source, Tao.

Excessive anger, resentment, rage, jealousy, frustration, or stress causes chi stagnation, which leads to thicker, acidic blood. This can manifest as dizziness, weakness, headaches, tinnitus, dry cracked nails, muscle cramps, indigestion, diarrhea, nausea, or jaundice. Chronic liver disharmony may lead to eye infections, failing vision, menstrual difficulties, arthritis, eczema, psoriasis, or cancer.

According to TCM, high winds are disturbing to the liver. In and of themselves, they can cause irritation and anger.

Wood is the Element of the liver and gallbladder. The season of wood is spring. The energetic nature of wood is energy expanding and growing — think of a tree expanding its roots and branches. The positive emotions of kindness and generosity are clear examples of energy expanding, of reaching out to help others.

The negative emotion of anger is also energy expanding; it's highly volatile. Anger unchecked expands into frustration, resentment, jealousy, or rage. It may expand into the psychological trait of overcriticalness. Mikio Sankey suggests it can become excessive compulsion, as in the type A personality hell-bent for success.[5]

The positive psychological traits of decisiveness, planning, and precision are energy expanding and growing; these relate to the gallbladder. The negative traits of the gallbladder are the opposite of growth: procrastination and inflexibility.

Specific Foods and Color to Soothe Anger and Its Variations

As mentioned before, eat fresh, locally grown, organic food as much as possible. Avoid canned, processed, irradiated, or genetically modified food. Include all five tastes and colors in your daily diet. Substitute a small amount of raw honey or 100 percent pure maple syrup for cane sugar. Our bodies need oil, but use it wisely in your diet. The best oils for the liver are raw organic butter, raw organic coconut oil, raw organic olive oil, and raw organic hemp oil. Avoid deep frying or prolonged frying. Cook lightly and quickly with coconut oil and use olive oil on salads and vegetables. Use organic raw butter on your bread and vegetables. Add raw organic hemp oil, which has omega-3 and omega-6 oils, to salads and vegetables; don't cook with it.

Spring is the season when the liver and gallbladder work the hardest. Sour foods and green foods support these organs. Many fruits are in the sour category: apples, berries, grapefruits, grapes, oranges, pears, lemons, and tomatoes. Organic flesh foods in the sour category are: freshwater fish, chicken, turkey, and meats. Organic fermented foods in the sour category are: bread (especially artisan-quality, unyeasted sourdough), raw nonvinegar pickles, sprouts, live culture yogurt, raw kefir, raw salted feta, raw (unpasteurized) sauerkraut, and homemade kombucha tea (made with raw honey). If your liver or gallbladder is very weak, it's best to minimize sour foods and emphasize salty and bitter foods instead. (See index for salty foods and bitter foods.)

Eating one or more servings of fermented food daily is a powerful way to enhance your liver and gallbladder, strengthen your digestion, boost your nutrition, and increase your immunity to diseases. Fermentation produces probiotics, healthy microflora, that travel to your small intestine and help to digest your food. Lactobacillus microflora generally produce most of the B complex vitamins. Acidophilus bifidus microflora produce B_{12}, folic acid, and butyrate. Organic raw milk, raw kefir, live culture yogurt, and raw feta cheese have both lactobacillus and bifidus microflora. Raw unpasteurized sauerkraut and its brine are loaded with lactobacilli and vitamin C.[6] It can be difficult to find these fermented, raw, unpasteurized foods in stores. Two of the books recommended in the Selected References of this book (in the "Nutrition" section), *Wild Fermentation* and *Nourishing Traditions*, give quick, easy recipes for these "longevity foods." You may be able to find these foods online as well.

Green foods contain chlorophyll and lutein, which aid detoxification, a major task of the liver and gallbladder network.[7] So include lightly cooked broccoli, bok choy, Chinese cabbage, collard greens, kale, and spinach in your diet. Keep in mind that raw spinach and raw, unfermented cabbage interfere with the absorption of iodine.[8]

Wearing green also supports your liver and gallbladder. Since wood is their element, walk in the woods, in a park, or along a tree-lined street frequently and appreciate the beauty and utility of trees. They're the lungs of our planet — they create oxygen and absorb carbon dioxide. They also provide shade and produce fruit and nuts. And they prevent erosion of the soil and provide us with material for, among other things, homes, wooden furniture, and wood sculpture.

Notes

1. Ursula K. Le Guin, *Lao Tzu: Tao Te Ching* (Boston: Shambhala, 1997), chap. 63, p. 81.

2. Ibid., chap. 27, p. 37.

3. Giovanni Maciocia, *The Foundations of Chinese Medicine* (Edinburgh: Churchill Livingstone, 1989), p. 78.

4. Ibid., p. 77–80.

5. Mikio Sankey, *Discern the Whisper: Esoteric Acupuncture*, vol. 2 (Inglewood, CA: Mountain Castle Publishing, 2002), p. 55.

6. Jack Bezian, interviews by Dena Saxer, March 25 and April 9, 2009, Santa Monica, CA. Jack is a master sourdough baker and fermentation expert.

7. Maoshing Ni, *Secrets of Self-Healing* (New York: Avery, 2008), p. 77.

8. Sally Fallon, with Mary G. Enig, *Nourishing Traditions*, 2nd ed. (Washington, DC: New Trends Publishing, 2001), p. 44.

CHAPTER 7

ARROGANCE, IMPATIENCE, CRUELTY, HATE, AND MANIA

ARROGANCE IS AN ATTITUDE characterized by feeling or acting superior to other people. It's not the same as taking pride in our work and expressing our genuine pleasure when we accomplish something in a skillful way. And it can be very subtle. We may treat someone kindly but in a condescending manner. We may assume we know all the answers in our area of expertise. Or we may privately believe that our mode of living, or our politics, or our spiritual practices are best for everyone. Of course, arrogance can be blatant, too, as when we denounce or punish those whose beliefs or practices diverge from ours.

Impatience with ourselves or others comes from not being aware of the dynamics of a situation. Every action, every interaction, has a rhythm, a natural energy flow. Although we may think we are saving time by being impatient, we are probably slowing down or compromising the completion of a task. The calm, aware person will hear the abrasive wheel, stop the motor, and oil it. The impatient one will force it forward and break the machine.

Hate and cruelty are extreme emotions and especially harmful to your heart, your Soul, and your Spirit. Mania, or overexcitement, is a heart imbalance that results from sudden, extreme joy or success.

The Valuable Messages of These Strong Emotions

He who stands on tiptoe is not steady.
He who strides cannot maintain the pace.
He who makes a show is not enlightened.
He who is self-righteous is not respected.
He who boasts achieves nothing.
He who brags will not endure.

Tao Te Ching[2]

If we are feeling arrogant, impatient, cruel, or hateful toward other people, this is a clear message that we are estranged from our enthusiasm, our gratitude, our trust, our compassion, our joy, and our love. These positive emotions are the natural expression of our Original Spirit, which connects us to Tao and resides in our heart.

As the proverb says, "Pride [arrogance] goeth before a fall!" When we puff ourselves up with importance because of our beliefs, our talents, our achievements, our possessions, or our looks, sooner or later we fall on our face — we make a major blunder. Reaching a position of power in any field of endeavor is a test of our character. The media love to highlight famous athletes, film stars, or elected officials — or their kids — who become addicted to drugs or commit crimes. We may not break the law or become junkies, but none of us are exempt from letting power go to our heads. Spiritual leaders, college professors, writers, accountants, nursery school teachers —

anyone can fall prey to arrogance. As parents, we may find that it's easy to cross the fine line between being firm and being overbearing. There's an implicit arrogance in demanding compliance from our children simply because we hold power over them.

Very few of us are deliberately cruel. When we are stressed, exhausted, or ill, we may say or do something unkind to someone who is pressuring us. Sometimes what we intend as a helpful comment to someone is perceived by him or her as hurtful or condescending. Even if our comment is the perfect solution to the problem, he or she may need to find that solution alone. As a general rule, it's best not to offer advice unless it's asked for — and even then we must tread lightly.

No one likes to lose face. Yet it may be necessary to criticize another person's actions or words. If possible, *first* find some aspect to praise, and then *gently* voice what needs to be changed. Dena at one time taught college courses in public speaking to working adults. At the beginning of a semester, about 90 percent of them would be fearful about speaking before the class. Speech researchers tell us that fear of public humiliation, especially in public speaking, is the second-most common fear, after death. Knowing this, Dena required alternating groups of students to verbally critique each speech after it was delivered. They were asked to follow the criteria taught in class and to first identify the specific strengths of the speech. Then they were asked to suggest specific improvements, always in a supportive way. This method worked beautifully for a few thousand students. The praise made them feel appreciated and validated; then they were able to hear and accept the "improvements." And, to their credit, almost all of them became noticeably more confident, more dynamic, and more informative in their speeches.

If you find yourself hating someone or some situation, or having cruel thoughts, it's time to back off and take a break. Quietly, by yourself, use the Six Healing Sounds and Releasing One Emotion practices to understand the reasons for your hate or cruelty and to find a way to transcend them. Sharing your concerns with a compassionate relative, friend, or counselor can be helpful. At any rate, you can't allow hate or cruelty to harm yourself or others.

Overexcitement or mania is a heart imbalance. Too much joy or success that comes on suddenly, without preparation, can upset your heart energy and spill over to all your internal organs. Some people have died from heart failure in response to too much happiness all at once. Manic depression, or bipolar disorder, is also an imbalance of heart energy.[1]

Changing Arrogance, Impatience, Cruelty, Hate, and Mania

God is a state of happiness, not a state of judgment.

Ronald Beesley[3]

Fear is really the cause of these troublesome emotions. Arrogance arises when we secretly or unconsciously judge ourselves as unworthy. So we put up a big front, to hide our poor self-esteem. Impatience occurs when we're afraid a project will not succeed. Hate and cruelty grow from the fear of being too vulnerable. And overexcitement comes from too much happiness all at once, making us fear that we don't deserve it.

The Six Healing Sounds, Inner Smile, and Releasing One Emotion practices help enormously in connecting with our Original Spirit, in our heart. Our heart will then speak to us. It may speak kinesthetically, letting us feel a sense of calmness and lightness when we consider beneficial actions and a sense of uneasiness and heaviness when we consider adverse actions. It may also communicate with images in our mind or even in words. It will guide us to those actions that create compassion, gratitude, trust, joy, and love.

The way to happiness and health requires us to face our deficiencies, learn from them, and then let them go. So if we find ourselves being arrogant, we forgive ourselves and then we correct it. The same with impatience, cruelty, hate, and overexcitement. The more we consciously correct ourselves, the easier it becomes to do. *And the less often we have to do it.*

Arrogance, Impatience, Cruelty, Hate, and Mania — Housed in Our Heart and Small Intestine

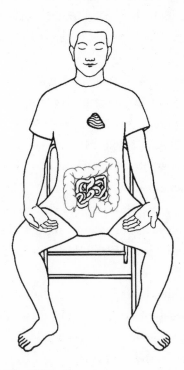

FIGURE 9: Heart and Small Intestine

When the troubling emotions of arrogance, impatience, cruelty, hate, and mania are not processed and transformed, they build up in the heart and small intestine. They weaken these organs and cause them to malfunction. They also weaken the positive emotions that reside there: enthusiasm, gratitude, trust, joy, compassion, and love.

Western medicine tells us that the heart is the first internal organ to develop in the fetus (a beautiful plan by Mother Nature). Anatomically, it's a muscular double pump that, in an adult, is about the size of our fist. It controls and regulates the circulation of blood through the blood vessels to all the cells of the body. In its one-way journey, away from the heart and lungs and back again, the blood delivers oxygen, nutrients, antibodies, and hormones, and it removes carbon dioxide and other metabolic wastes. It's constantly working for us — it never takes a vacation.

Western medicine describes the small intestine as a curled-up tube measuring about twenty feet long that is the main organ of digestion and absorption of food. It receives partially digested food from the stomach and then alters it chemically by means of digestive juices and enzymes. This converts the food into the body's basic requirements of simple sugars, amino acids, and fatty acids. Next the small intestine absorbs these nutrients into the bloodstream and sends them to the liver for immediate use or storage. It sends the wastewater and solid particles to the large intestine, which absorbs the water and salts and excretes the solids.

Traditional Chinese Medicine calls the heart the "chief" or "director" of all the internal organs. It governs the blood and controls the blood vessels. It manifests in the complexion and controls the tongue, the taste buds, and the sweat.

Spiritually, the heart is the leader of our being. It houses Original Spirit, our direct connection to Tao (God, Source, and so on). Original Spirit can also be called Shen. Shen has two aspects, ordinary mind and Higher Mind. Ordinary mind includes memory, intelligence, thinking, and emotional abilities. Higher Mind includes the sum total of the functions of the entire spiritual team composed of the heart Shen; the liver Soul, Hun; the spleen Spirit, Yi; the lung Soul, Po; and the kidney Spirit, Zhi. Heart Shen leads, coordinates, and harmonizes the team. Higher Shen is the coach, a player, and also all the players working together.

TCM says that the small intestine rules the separation of the "pure" from the "waste." Psychologically, it says, the small intestine rules the ability to discern relevant issues with clarity.[4] In other words, it separates the useful from the extraneous.

The tongue is the sense organ connected energetically to the heart. A normal, pale red tongue and normal taste buds reflect a balanced, healthy heart. Distortion in tongue color, shape, or taste buds reflects a heart imbalance from arrogance, impatience, cruelty, hate, mania, or some other external cause. In relation to the tongue, heart imbalance can also manifest as speech problems, such as stuttering, or in incessant talking or inappropriate laughter.

Excessive heat from the sun is harmful to the heart and small intestine. It can trigger impatience or overexcitement.

Chronic arrogance, impatience, mania, cruelty, or hate weakens the heart and small intestine and causes them to malfunction. Symptoms of heart malfunction include heart murmurs, chest pain, weakness, dizziness, insomnia, coma, stroke, and heart arrest. Symptoms of small intestine malfunction include indigestion, nausea, cramps, diarrhea, constipation, and malnutrition.

Fire is the element of the heart and small intestine. The season when they work the hardest is summer. The energetic actions of fire are energy rising and growing. We can see these actions in both the positive and negative emotions. Enthusiasm, gratitude, joy, trust, compassion, and love are ascending emotions — they raise us up;

they make us feel taller and more wonderful. Arrogance, impatience, mania, hate, and cruelty also rise and grow in intensity until we lose our balance and fall.

Specific Foods and Colors to Alleviate Arrogance, Impatience, Cruelty, Hate, and Mania

Eat fresh, locally grown, organic food as much as possible. Avoid canned, processed, irradiated, or genetically modified food. Include all five tastes and colors in your daily diet. Bitter is the taste that supports the heart and small intestine. Most Americans eat few or no bitter foods. Could this be related to the fact that heart disease is the number one killer in the United States? Bitter foods include artichoke, asparagus, avocado, bok choy, broccoli, cauliflower, celery, dandelion greens, leeks, mushrooms, mustard greens, rutabagas, and turnips. Avocado, broccoli, cauliflower, and celery can be eaten raw for optimal vitamins, minerals, and enzymes. Cook the others lightly and briefly on a medium flame in a small amount of water. Or stir-fry quickly in organic raw coconut oil or olive oil; then add a little water and simmer briefly. This will retain most of their vitamins, minerals, and enzymes.

If your heart or small intestine is very weak, it's best to minimize the bitter foods and emphasize sour and sweet foods. (See index for these.)

Red is the color that nourishes the heart and small intestine. Red foods contain the antioxidant lycopene.[5] Include in your diet beets, radishes, raspberries, red cabbage, tomatoes, and a small amount of red bell or hot peppers. Organic grated raw beets in your salads will lubricate your intestines, nourish your blood, and provide hydrochloric acid for digesting proteins.

Wearing red clothes is fun and energizing, and most people enjoy seeing other people wearing red. However, if you're overexcited, it's best to cool down with blue, green, or black clothes.

Appreciate the element of fire in your life. We need it to cook food on stoves, outdoor grills, or in fireplaces. We warm our homes with furnaces or wood-burning stoves. And fire is crucial in transforming and shaping metal for so many of our modern necessities, such as manufacturing machines, agricultural machines, building foundations, appliances, electronic devices, cars, trucks, trains, planes, tools, pots, tableware, and musical instruments.

Of course, our most important fire is the sun, which sustains all life on earth. We suggest giving thanks every day for our sun. If you do this at sunrise or sunset while *turning your closed eyes to the sun*, it will give you additional Cosmic Chi energy. Getting some sun for twenty minutes every day when possible, preferably before 10 AM or after 2 PM, boosts your Life Force Chi, your Internal Organ Chi, and your Sexual Chi.

Notes

1. Giovanni Maciocia, *The Foundations of Chinese Medicine* (Edinburgh: Churchill Livingstone, 1989), pp. 73, 210–11.
2. Gia-Fu Feng and Jane English, *Lao Tsu: Tao Te Ching* (New York: Vintage Books, 1972), chap. 24.
3. Ronald P. Beesley, *The Path of Esoteric Truthfulness* (Kent, England: White Lodge Publications, 1976), p. 104.
4. Maciocia, *Foundations of Chinese Medicine*, p. 115.
5. Maoshing Ni, *Secrets of Self-Healing* (New York: Avery, 2008), p. 78.

CHAPTER 8

WORRY, ANXIETY, SHAME, GUILT, AND SELF-PITY

You can always find something *to worry about!*

Roz, a Jewish mother

WORRY AND ANXIETY ARE FEAR-BASED EMOTIONS. They project negative outcomes for our problems. Worry is certainly milder than anxiety, but it's still destructive if it's habitual. Anxiety is so powerful that it can spill over from one difficult situation to other, unrelated ones. It can spread and become a jittery, suspicious approach to all of life. Sadly and ironically, focusing on catastrophe is more likely to attract catastrophe to us.

Frequent worry and anxiety are emotional cancers that eat away our peace of mind and our enjoyment of life. They also compromise our physical health. Chi kung and Traditional Chinese Medicine say that anxiety and worry can literally "eat us up" — they consume the life force, the chi, of our digestion and absorption organs, the stomach, spleen, and pancreas.

What Causes Worry or Anxiety?

The most obvious source of these learned emotions is our parents. They may teach us directly when they are overly concerned about our physical safety, reacting with alarm at every minor tumble. Or we may learn these emotions unconsciously if our parents themselves are habitual worriers or anxiety-prone. In some unfortunate cases, a parent's rejection or abuse of a child creates a realistic dread of emotional or physical pain that is later projected onto the child's adult relationships.

On a deeper level, the process of "civilizing" children is a major culprit. Many of us were taught to disregard or deny our spontaneous emotions of anger, fear, or sadness in favor of socially approved ones. Be nice! Don't be nasty! Grow up — don't be a scaredy-cat! Stop crying! What are you, a baby? This last one is, for many boys, the ultimate put-down.

Looking beyond the family for sources of worry and anxiety, we can see that our materialistic society thrives on creating fear. The media, advertising, and many elected officials deliberately highlight possible dangers, diseases, and disasters. Get people worried, really worried, and they will buy your newspapers, your escapist TV shows, your tranquilizers, and your wars.

Living in Our Heads

When worry or anxiety takes over, we become unbalanced. We live in our heads. Our minds become "monkey minds," endlessly chattering to us about dire consequences that will probably never happen. We waste our life-force energy, our chi, on useless thoughts.

Here are some suggestions for breaking the worry or anxiety cycle. If you have a genuine problem to resolve, adopt a calm, positive attitude; this will help you sort out the relevant details. The Six

Healing Sounds are remarkably helpful for quickly creating calmness and clarity. Undistracted by fear, we can look objectively at possible solutions. We can discuss these with our family or friends. We can consult an expert, if necessary. If a clear solution doesn't appear for a while, probably some crucial information is missing. Dena's favorite reminder to herself at a time like this is: "Not all the info is in. When you know the answer, you know it!" You feel that kinesthetic sense of certainty.

The Ultimate Authority

If you do what is needed in the moment,
as guided by your heart, you will get what you need.

Michael Morgan, spiritual teacher

Dena first heard this profound saying in 1993 and took it to heart. She found that listening to her heart's messages is the best way to live a joyful, productive, peaceful, healthy life, without becoming a hermit. The only certainties in anyone's life are change, transformation, and our personal direct line to Original Spirit, in our heart. Original Spirit is our ultimate authority.

We're speaking here about trust. If we ask for and follow our heart's guidance, we will never go wrong. We will be amazed at the daily hunches, the synchronicities, and the good fortune we attract. We will overcome every obstacle, or we'll learn a valuable lesson we needed to learn. Often we don't understand the reasons for adversity until some time has passed. If we trust our Original Spirit, what seems like a disaster may eventually turn into an amazing blessing.

Worry and anxiety are symptoms of a lack of trust. And which internal organ is the home of trust? The heart, of course. To increase our ability to trust, the Six Healing Sounds, Inner Smile, and Releasing

One Emotion practices are superb tools for strengthening our trust and transforming worry and anxiety.

Shame, Guilt, and Self-Pity

The emotion of shame is a serious problem for many people. Learning to ignore or repress our true feelings creates a deep sense of frustration. It may cause us to feel unworthy due to our natural responses. Shame may be the hidden reason for a persistent fear of failure that manifests as worry or anxiety.

Guilt is self-reproach for having done something harmful to others or to oneself. Guilt can be a healthy response when it moves us to change our wrong behavior. But it's an emotional cancer when we imagine or exaggerate our fault, or if we allow it to continue to haunt us. If we did something wrong, we need to make amends if possible. Then we need to forgive ourselves and move forward.

Self-pity is the "poor me" syndrome — believing that adverse events in our lives are caused by outside forces that are arbitrarily harming us. It's seeing ourselves as unfortunate victims of circumstances beyond our control. The Taoist way is to respond courageously and positively to everything we encounter in our lives. If we have attracted illness, financial loss, or other misfortunes, these are opportunities for us to learn from our trials and grow. These are opportunities to change the underlying imbalances or disharmonies that are blocking our health, happiness, or prosperity. In any crisis, if we trust our Original Spirit, in our heart, it will guide us, moment by moment, to the most beneficial actions. As the Sufi poet Jelaluddin Rumi advised back in the thirteenth century:

> *Those of you who are scattered,*
> *simplify your worrying lives. There is one*

righteousness: Water the fruit trees,
and don't water the thorns. Be generous
to what nurtures the spirit. . . .
Don't honor what causes
dysentery and knotted up tumors.[1]

Worry, Anxiety, Shame, Guilt, and Self-Pity — Housed in Our Stomach, Spleen, and Pancreas

FIGURE 10: Stomach, Spleen, and Pancreas

These troubling emotions make their home in the stomach, spleen, and pancreas. These organs also store the positive emotion of openness, and the psychological traits of stability, fairness, honesty, and powerful intention. Frequent worry, anxiety, and their variations impair these desirable qualities.

Western medicine describes the stomach as a muscular sac shaped like a gourd. Its function is to liquefy, churn, and partially digest food and drink received from the mouth and esophagus. The stomach secretes gastric juice containing hydrochloric acid and enzymes. The acid softens connective tissue in meat, kills bacteria, and activates the enzyme that begins digesting protein. Alternate contractions and relaxations in the lower part of the stomach mash and mix the food with the gastric juice and mucus until it's a soupy paste. The stomach then squeezes the liquefied food into the small intestine to complete its digestion and absorption.

The spleen filters out old, worn-out red blood cells and destroys them. It forms white blood cells, which destroy bacteria and viruses. It also produces antibodies against specific diseases. The spleen is an emergency reservoir of red blood cells in case of hemorrhaging or other contingencies.

The pancreas secretes insulin to regulate blood sugar levels. It produces pancreatic juice with digestive enzymes, which it sends into the small intestine to digest fats, proteins, and carbohydrates. It also produces an alkaline fluid for neutralizing the acidity of food in the small intestine.

TCM and chi kung view the stomach's role as that of transforming ingested food and drink by fermentation. The stomach is the origin of fluids in the body. The stomach and spleen control the transportation of food essences, and they are both origins of chi in the body. A strong stomach is regarded as essential for healing any disease. The stomach is the yang partner to the yin spleen.[2]

In TCM, the spleen is crucial for digestion and for the production of Life Force Chi and blood. The spleen extracts food chi from ingested food and drink and sends it throughout the body to nourish all the tissues. Specifically, it sends food chi up to the lungs to form gathering chi, and to the heart to form blood. The spleen energetically controls the muscles and the four limbs: spleen chi must be strong enough to send food chi to these areas, or they will be weak. The spleen chi connects to the mouth and lips; if the spleen is healthy, the sense of taste will be good and the lips will be moist and red.[3] The spleen dislikes dampness. It is harmed by a damp environment and by wearing damp clothes.[4]

Spiritually, the spleen houses the Power of Intention Spirit, or Yi in Chinese. Intention influences our ability to concentrate and focus on what's essential. No wonder chi kung and TCM emphasize the importance of a fresh, natural, balanced diet. How can we think clearly if we're eating junk food, food with toxic preservatives, or poorly prepared food?

Older Chinese medical books ignore the pancreas. Some modern ones link it to the spleen, calling the pair the spleen-pancreas.

Earth is the element of the stomach, spleen, and pancreas. The energetic nature of earth is stabilizing and grounding — which is exactly what is missing from our heady, chaotic, stressful Western lifestyle. If our earth energy is compromised by excessive worrying, anxiety, shame, guilt, or self-pity, we are likely to experience one or more of these symptoms: belching, hiccups, acid reflux, poor appetite, nausea, diarrhea, fatigue, muscle flaccidity, or muscle weakness. The Healing Sounds and Inner Smile are superb for improving our grounding and stability.

Specific Foods and Colors to Alleviate Worry, Anxiety, Shame, Guilt, and Self-Pity

Since we're focusing on the digestive and nourishing organs, let's talk in more detail about eating. Excellent nutrition is essential for emotional, physical, and spiritual health. An important way to maximize the nutritional value of our food is to approach the entire process with attention, love, and reverence. Where we buy our food, how carefully we select it, how we store it, how we prepare it, how we serve it, and how we eat it — all these details contribute to the food's chi, its visual appeal, its scent and taste, and its nutrition. Think of eating as a sacred act — it sustains our lives. Every single meal is a gift from Tao, the Source, as well as from the sun, the earth, the rain, and a staggering number of people: farmers, pickers, distributors, market workers, and others.

Avoid canned, packaged, processed, or genetically modified food. As much as possible, eat fresh, organic, locally grown food. Your very best choice for nutrition, taste, safety, and economy is to grow your own fruits and vegetables. If this is not an option, go to a farmers' market with an organic section. The food will have been picked one or two days before, and you'll have an opportunity to meet the people who grow or pick your food. Most organic farmers and their helpers are proud that they provide healthful and nutritious food. That positive vibration goes into your food. For other items, shop at a health food co-op or an independent health food store. Read all the labels carefully; even these stores sell many nonorganic, sugar-added, processed foods. For each day's menu, include items covering all five tastes and a variety of colors, especially raw or lightly cooked greens.

When you get home, take vegetables and fruits out of their plastic bags. Place unripened fruits in a bowl, and tomatoes on a plate, stem side up. Wrap the rest in waxed paper, put them in containers or back in the plastic bags they came in, and store them in the refrigerator. This will better preserve their nutrients and freshness.

What about raw foods? Most practitioners of TCM recommend eating mostly cooked food, believing that too much raw food weakens the immune system. However, research by the late Dr. Edward Howell, a noted pioneer in the study of enzymes, found that a diet primarily made up of cooked foods led to an enlarged pancreas, a shortened life span, illness, and poor resistance to stress.[5] We suspect that coping with the stresses of modern living may require more energy than a largely cooked diet provides.

A number of people, especially young people, have switched to a predominantly raw food diet because raw foods have more vitamins, minerals, and digestive enzymes. If you are very yang and have abundant chi and strong digestive fire, you may flourish with mostly raw foods. A raw diet may also be useful for a short-term cleansing. Otherwise, we suggest that you include some raw food each day and see how you feel. It's excellent for overcoming constipation. Keep in mind the principle of balancing yin and yang: since raw food is very yin, start by eating raw foods at lunchtime, which is the most yang part of the day. As your body adjusts to raw food, you may wish to increase the amount, again assessing its effects. However, as Sally Fallon and Mary Enig point out, "there are no traditional diets composed exclusively of raw foods. Even in the tropics . . . [people] build a fire every day to cook their foods. . . . In general, whole grains, legumes and certain types of vegetables should be cooked."[6] When you cook vegetables, retain their nutrients by steaming them or stir-frying them lightly in a small amount of water or olive or coconut oil, so they remain crisp and retain most of their color.

Also, you can increase your digestive enzymes and strengthen your immune system by eating some organic fermented food each day, such as raw unpasteurized sauerkraut, raw nonvinegar pickles, live culture yogurt, raw kefir, miso, tamari, and artisan-quality unyeasted sourdough bread. (See index: Fermented Foods.)

Taoist chef and teacher Michael Brosnahan taught us that a good cook "makes love to the food as he or she prepares it." Admire its vibrant colors, unique shapes, and various textures. When you cut vegetables, use an excellent quality, sharpened knife and a good cutting board. Slide or roll your knife through your vegetables in a graceful rhythm; don't hack at them. Cook your food with care and attention. Arrange your food attractively on the plate. When cherished by you in this way, your food will return your love with enhanced nutrition and exquisite tastes.

If we take a few moments before eating to give silent or verbal thanks for the blessings of each meal, we further improve both our digestion and the chi of the food. A quick way to include all those involved is to give thanks to Tao, or God (or whatever you call the Source), and all the providers and preparers. When eating out, a discreet expression of gratitude gives us "more chi for our cash." Even if we never cook, we can choose restaurants that take pride in healthy and appealing food.

There are also many individual cooks and private companies who prepare and deliver healthy, organic, beautiful meals. To find them, go online or ask at your local health food store.

For excellent digestion, it's important to eat slowly and enjoy your food. Take small bites and chew each one thoroughly, mixing it with lots of saliva, until it turns liquid and glides down your throat. Saliva begins the digestive process, especially of carbohydrates. Obesity is a serious problem in the United States. Consider eating only until you are 70 percent or 80 percent full. This worked for the ancient Taoists, who were noted for longevity. Avoid extremely hot or extremely cold foods; they harm the digestive organs. Ice cream, iced drinks, and ice water extinguish our digestive fire.

Late summer is the season when our stomach, spleen, and pancreas are working the hardest. They prefer food cooked lightly, steamed, or boiled in a little water, with few seasonings and a mild taste. Support them in late summer, and all seasons, by eating yellow

or orange foods. These contain carotenoids, which support the digestive system.[7] The foods that provide carotenoids include apricots,
cantaloupes (eat these separately from other foods), carrots, pineap-
ples, pumpkins, summer squash, and winter squash. Foods that grow
under the ground are also beneficial — they're grounding! These
include potatoes (especially red ones), rutabagas, sweet potatoes,
turnips, and yams.[8]

The taste that alleviates worry, anxiety, shame, guilt, and self-
pity by strengthening the stomach, spleen, and pancreas is sweet-
ness. Please don't run amok in your local bakery, gorging on double
chocolate cake and lemon meringue pie. Or stock your freezer with
ten tubs of gourmet ice cream. These temptations are sweetened with
processed cane sugar, which not only harms our teeth and makes our
blood more acidic but also is the favorite food of bacteria, viruses,
and molds growing in our bodies. According to Mikio Sankey, cane
sugar also lowers our spiritual vibration.[9] (So eating sugar-sweetened
foods probably reduces the power of the Healing Sounds and Inner
Smile.) We crave sweet foods when our personal lives lack the sweet-
ness of caring relationships. It's best to eliminate processed cane sugar
altogether. Substitute *a small amount* of organic raw honey or 100
percent pure maple syrup. For a healthy snack, eat a few organic dates
or dried figs. And rely on the multitude of delicious, mildly sweet
foods listed in the next few paragraphs to satisfy your sweet tooth.
After a little retraining, your taste buds will reject extremely sweet
junk foods.

Many other healthy foods are in the sweet category, including vegetables such as corn, cabbage, cucumber, eggplant, jicama, lettuce,
peas, shiitake mushrooms, and string beans. Cabbage is best eaten as
raw unpasteurized sauerkraut or cooked; plain raw cabbage inhibits
the absorption of iodine.[10] Whole grains are considered sweet, and

these include buckwheat, millet, oats, brown rice, spelt, and wheat. Wheat is a common allergen. It's usually well tolerated in artisan quality sourdough bread, because a long fermentation process destroys its gluten, which causes the allergic reaction. Amaranth, rye, quinoa, and red quinoa (delicious!) are both sweet and bitter; both types of quinoa must be washed with at least three changes of filtered water to lose their bitterness; use a fine mesh strainer to remove each change of water. Sweet legumes include adzuki beans, black beans, chickpeas, lentils, mung beans, black-eyed peas, and soybeans. Soybeans are very hard to digest. Go easy on soy products such as tofu and protein powders; they are very high in phytic acid, an enzyme inhibitor that blocks the absorption of calcium, magnesium, zinc, and other minerals. Raw organic hemp powder is a better source of protein.

All whole grains and beans contain phytic acid, but presoaking them neutralizes it. So first wash them a few times, with the help of a fine-mesh strainer, and then soak whole grains and beans in filtered water and a little sea salt for eight to twelve hours. Then *discard the soak water* and replace it with filtered water, and cook.[11]

Fresh, raw, unprocessed seeds and nuts are sweet; they should be eaten in small quantities. They also contain phytic acid, so they, too, should be *soaked in filtered water for a few hours or overnight*. These include almonds, brazil nuts, chestnuts, coconuts, pumpkin seeds, sesame seeds (lightly roasted in a frying pan or as tahini), sunflower seeds, and walnuts.

Chocolate, even if organic, is high in oxalic acid, which blocks the absorption of calcium, and high in theobromine, a caffeinelike substance; in addition, most chocolate contains sugar. If you have a chocolate "habit," it may reflect a need for magnesium. Get your magnesium from whole grains, beans, vegetables, nuts, or seeds. Satisfy your sweet tooth with sweet fruits.

If your stomach, spleen, or pancreas are very weak, it's best to min-imize the sweet foods and emphasize bitter and spicy foods. (See index.)

Wearing yellow, gold, or orange will strengthen your digestive organs and lift your spirits. Friends and strangers alike are apt to smile and compliment you when you wear these cheerful, sunny colors.

To improve your grounding and stability, and to dissipate worry, anxiety, shame, or self-pity, spend more time in nature. Talk a walk in the country or a park. Do some gardening or at least grow house-plants. Taking care of a pet is a wonderful grounding experience. And every day, we can give thanks to Mother Earth for nurturing us.

Notes

1. Jelaluddin Rumi, "A Basket of Fresh Bread," in *The Essential Rumi*, trans. Coleman Barks (Edison, NJ: Castle Books, 1997), p. 256.

2. Giovanni Maciocia, *The Foundations of Chinese Medicine* (Edinburgh: Churchill Livingstone, 1989), pp. 111–114.

3. Ibid., pp. 89–93.

4. Ted J. Kaptchuk, *The Web That Has No Weaver* (New York: Congdon and Weed, 1983), pp. 124–125.

5. Sally Fallon, with Mary G. Enig, *Nourishing Traditions*, 2nd ed. (Washington, DC: New Trends Publishing, 2001), p. 47.

6. Ibid., p. 47.

7. Maoshing Ni, *Secrets of Self-Healing* (New York: Avery, 2008), p. 77.

8. Paul Pitchford, *Healing with Whole Foods: Oriental Traditions and Modern Nutrition* (Berkeley, CA: North Atlantic Books, 1993), p. 300.

9. Mikio Sankey, *Discern the Whisper: Esoteric Acupuncture*, vol. 2 (Inglewood, CA: Mountain Castle Publishing, 2002), p. 46.

10. Fallon and Enig, *Nourishing Traditions*, p. 44.

11. Pitchford, *Healing with Whole Foods*, p. 418.

Part Three

THE SIX HEALING SOUNDS

CHAPTER 9

AN INTRODUCTION TO THE HEALING SOUNDS

TO RELEASE AND TRANSFORM TROUBLING EMOTIONS, the Six Healing Sounds integrate four modalities: sound, arm movement, visualized color, and intentional smiling. The sounds release the unwanted emotions. The arm movements activate the meridians, or energy channels, of the affected organs, increasing the flow of chi. The visualized colors nourish these organs and support their positive emotions. Smiling to these organs creates a feeling of gratitude for their functions. Each of these four methods can be a powerful transformer of turbulent emotions — and together they are amazing!

A New Theory

A surgeon studying with Mantak Chia reported that patients who die of heart attacks have hearts that look like they've been cooked! In Traditional Chinese Medicine, the heart is covered with a protective membrane, or sac, called the pericardium; this sac absorbs heat and releases it through its meridians (energy pathways) to the skin, preventing the heart from overheating and malfunctioning. These two ideas, and Mantak Chia's own intuition and body awareness, led him to the following theory: that the recurrent painful emotions that are denied or repressed cause the fascia, the membranes enclosing corresponding internal organs, to overheat, contract, and stick to these organs, in this way blocking the normal cooling process. The overheated organ malfunctions and causes disease. Eventually, the heat spreads to other organs and to the muscles, causing further problems. When the Six Healing Sounds are practiced regularly, in the correct order, excess heat is released through the esophagus, and the organs and whole body are restored to their optimal temperature.

Signs of Tension Leaving

When we do the Sounds, we may sometimes yawn, burp, or pass gas. Or our eyes may tear and our saliva increase. Some people may have loose bowel movements because their bodies are cleansing themselves of toxins that may have accumulated for years. These are all positive signs: we are releasing negative emotions and, possibly, excess heat.

Another beneficial sign is greater physical flexibility. The range of movement in our arms, neck, shoulders, shoulder blades, and spine will increase as our muscles lose some of their tension. Feldenkrais therapist and Taoist teacher Joyce Gayheart taught her clients with back problems to do the kidney sound to help increase their spinal flexibility.

The Order of the Sounds

Chi kung and TCM view each emotion and its paired organs as connected to a season of the year. In this season, those organs are working the hardest and so are more vulnerable to emotional or physical stress. The Sounds are most effective when done in the natural order of the seasons: fall, winter, spring, summer, late summer. This is the order of the Creation Cycle, explained in chapter 2.

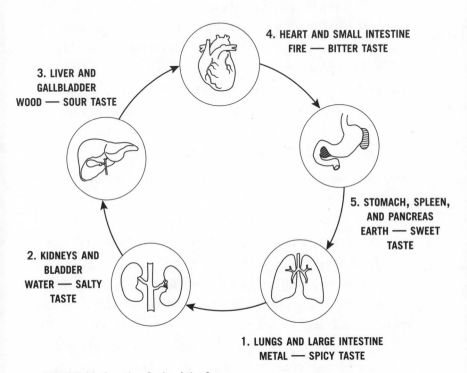

4. HEART AND SMALL INTESTINE
FIRE — BITTER TASTE

3. LIVER AND
GALLBLADDER
WOOD — SOUR TASTE

5. STOMACH, SPLEEN,
AND PANCREAS
EARTH — SWEET
TASTE

2. KIDNEYS AND
BLADDER
WATER — SALTY
TASTE

1. LUNGS AND LARGE INTESTINE
METAL — SPICY TASTE

FIGURE 11: Creation Cycle of the Organs

Generally, we repeat each Sound three times, six times, or more. Taoism favors multiples of threes, as in the three sources of external energy called "the Three Pure Ones": Universal Energy, Cosmic Energy, and Earth Energy. However, when an emotion and its organs are in their season, we increase the number of repetitions to six, twelve, or more to give them extra support. For example, sadness and depression are most prevalent in the fall, because the lungs and large intestine are working hardest then. So, in the fall, we do double the number of sadness-lung sounds, relative to the other sounds.

It's always optimal to do the whole sequence of Six Healing Sounds one or more times each day. But if you have one troubling emotion running rampant, or if you have a related physical symptom, you'll get relief by repeating the appropriate sound by itself many times. If, for example, you're depressed, do the lung sound until you feel lighter and happier. You can also do the Releasing One Emotion practice, concentrating on sadness. And if your lungs are stressed by a cold or flu, do the lung sound until your lungs or nose feel clearer.

When to Do the Six Healing Sounds

After the initial learning period, it will take you about twenty to thirty minutes to do the Six Healing Sounds. When you do them is not crucial. What is crucial is that you do them regularly. The quickest and most profound results come from daily practice. As Mantak Chia says, you do it — you get it; you don't do it — you don't get it!

Most people prefer to do the Six Sounds at night, before sleep. This promotes a deep, peaceful sleep; many people have cured insomnia this way. Doing the Sounds in the morning is also excellent; it will improve your entire day. If you have a physical exercise program, do the Sounds right after you finish it. If you do heavy exercises such as running, playing tennis or basketball, or dancing, doing the Sounds immediately afterward will release any excess heat. If you have a particularly challenging task ahead, doing the Sounds beforehand will help you carry it out in the best possible way. You're likely to astound yourself with your tact and graciousness.

CHAPTER 10

THE SIX HEALING SOUNDS PRACTICE, STEP-BY-STEP

IF YOU DON'T FEEL ANY TROUBLING EMOTION when you tune into a particular internal organ, either you don't have a problem with that emotion, or you're not yet aware of it. If you feel some *physical* imbalance or constriction in a particular organ, this could be caused by external factors, such as extreme climate, poor diet, environmental toxins, a previous injury, and so on. Regardless of whether you do or do not feel an emotion or an imbalance in one or more organs, you should still do all six sounds. This will keep all your emotions, your body, and your chi in balance.

The power of the Healing Sounds is in the sensory, physical experience, *not* the cerebral understanding of them. So, once you've learned the six parts, concentrate on making the sounds, doing the arm movements, smiling to the relevant organs, imagining the colored lights, and feeling the energetic release of the emotional or physical imbalances. Don't worry about remembering all the particular names of the painful emotions or even the positive ones. Be in the now of what happens in your body. When the emotions or their messages are ready, you will feel a kinesthetic nudge, or receive an image or a verbal insight.

Preparation

Wait at least an hour after eating, with this exception: If you're having digestive discomfort, you can immediately do a series of the fifth sound, *HOOOOOO*, until you feel relief. To do the entire Six Healing Sounds practice, make sure you won't be interrupted for thirty minutes or so. Once you've learned it, it may take only twenty minutes — or longer if you wish to deepen your practice. Wear loose-fitting, comfortable clothes — natural fabrics, like cotton, silk, or wool are best for chi flow. Stretch fabrics that are at least 70 percent natural are okay. Tight clothes restrict our chi. Wired bras do the same and may be related to the high incidence of breast cancer. Choose a warm, quiet spot. Turn off your phone. Dim the lights. Take off your watch and jewelry and loosen your belt. Select a straight-backed chair that allows your feet to rest on the floor. For comfort, put a pillow on the seat.

A Quick Standing Warm-Up

Unless you are already warmed up from your exercise routine, it's best to do a quick warm-up before doing the Six Healing Sounds. The following standing warm-up will get your chi activated and flowing, so that the Sounds will be even more effective.

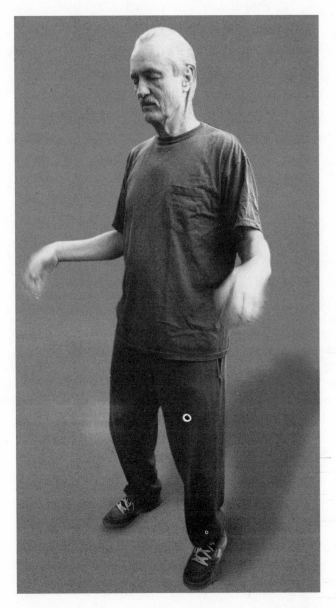

1. Keeping both feet on the floor, shake your whole body vigorously. Make a silly sound. Do this for one or two minutes.

2.   *Gently* hit the top of your head with your fists twelve or more
     times.

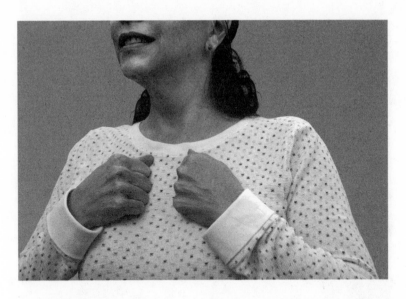

3. Hit your thymus gland area with alternate fists twelve or more times.

4. Slap your lungs with your palms twelve or more times. Women
   should slap their chests in a circle around their breasts.

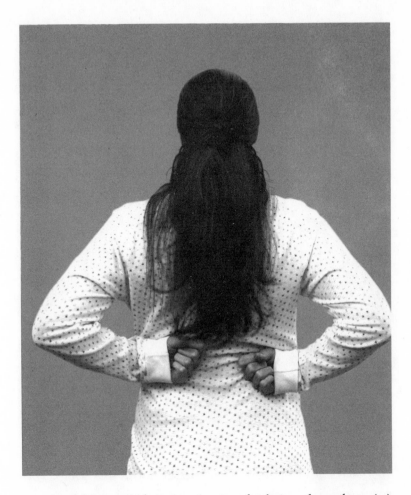

5. *Gently* hit your kidney area (on your back, just above the waist) with your fists twelve or more times. Then, with your palms, massage that area. Then rest your palms there and warm that area.

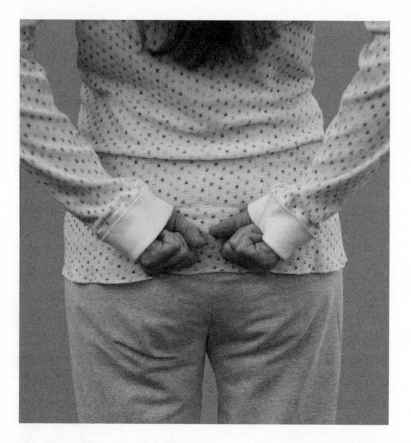

6. *Gently* hit your sacrum (above your tailbone) with your fists twelve or more times. Then massage it with your palms. Then rest your palms there and warm that area.

7. Place your palms on your belly. Laugh out loud using the sound *ha*. Feel your belly expand when you laugh. Then laugh like a chicken. Finally, laugh like a dog. Laughing activates your lymphatic system, liver, and thymus gland, which improves your immunity to disease.

8. Close your eyes and breathe silently through your nose into your belly. Feel it expand when you inhale, and contract when you exhale.

The Six Healing Sounds Practice

Sit on the edge of your chair, freeing the genital area, and keep your eyes open. Move your legs comfortably apart, and put your feet solidly on the floor. Keep your back straight, but not rigid.

Sound #1: Sadness into Courage

A. Always begin the Sounds with the lungs and large intestine, whose season is fall. Sadness and depression reside in these organs. Start by getting in touch with your lungs: close your eyes and put your hands on your rib cage. Inhale slowly through your nose. Exhale through your nose. Notice if you feel any sadness, depression, constriction, or other physical imbalance in your lungs. If you do, ask for the message of this feeling. The answer may come immediately or at some other time. When you know the message, let its wisdom guide your future actions.

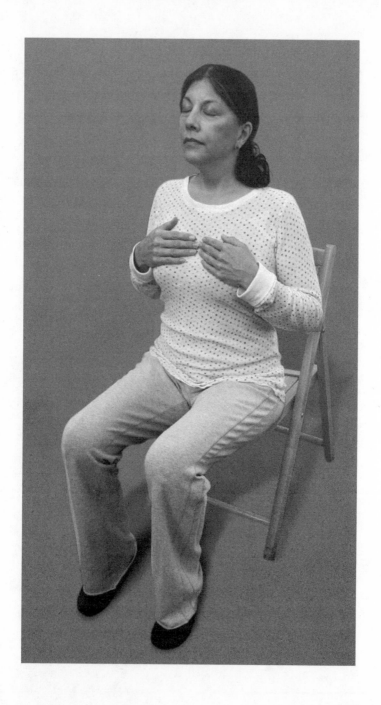

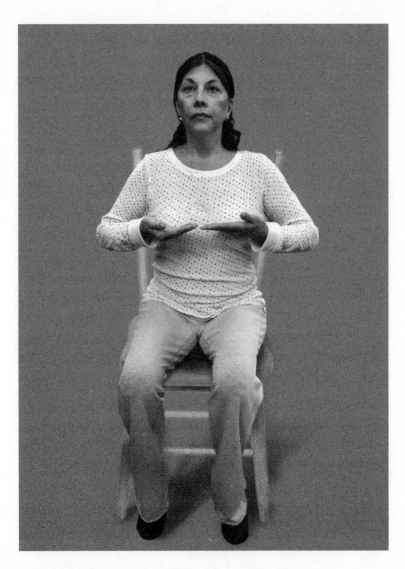

B. Now open your eyes. Inhale again deeply through your nose as you slowly move your hands a few inches away from your chest, turn your palms up, and raise your arms up toward your head.

C. Bring your palms above your head and rotate them to face the ceiling, holding them about six inches apart. Gently press upward with the heels of your palms; gently bend your elbows and press them out, away from the body. Bend your head back as far as is comfortable. Feel a gentle stretch from your palms to your elbows to your shoulders to the area of your lungs.

D. With eyes still open, exhale slowly, softly, and evenly, making the sound *SSSSS* (breath only, not vocalized) until you have exhaled all of your original breath. Visualize any sadness, depression, constriction, or imbalance leaving your mouth like a cloudy gray substance going into the earth to be transformed. (Don't worry about polluting Mother Earth. She transforms our negative energy into positive energy.)

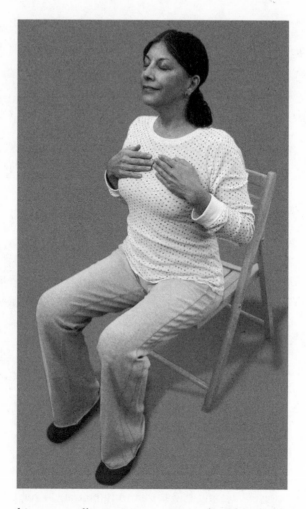

E. Breathing normally now, rotate your palms down, release your shoulders, and slowly float your hands back to cover your lungs. Close your eyes and *smile*, inwardly and outwardly, to your lungs and large intestine: feel grateful for their vital work in respiration and elimination. Then, still smiling, with every breath imagine you are breathing into these organs a brilliant *white light*, for a total of three or six breaths.

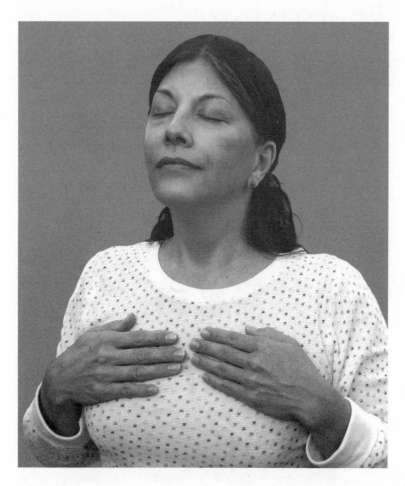

F. Repeat steps A through E for a total of three or six times. After
    each sound repetition, return your hands to your chest, covering
    your lungs.

        After your last repetition, sense that your lungs and large intes-
    tine are larger, softer, moister, and spongier. Sadness, depression,
    constriction, or imbalance have been released. Courage, right
    action, and letting go have been increased.

        If the season is fall, do double the number of *SSSSSS* sounds.

Sound #2: Fear into Gentleness

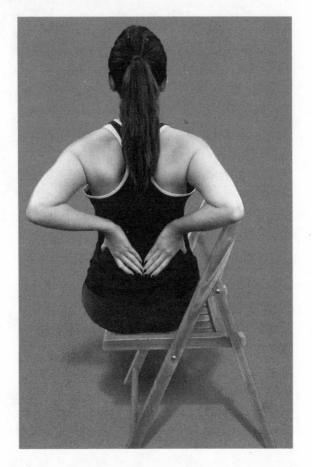

A. Fear and nervousness reside in the kidneys and bladder, whose season is winter. Connect to the kidneys by placing your hands on your back, just above the waist. Notice if you feel any fear, nervousness, constriction, or imbalance in your kidneys. If you do, ask for the message of this feeling.

B. Now open your eyes and bring your ankles and knees together. Inhale slowly and deeply through your nose as you sweep your arms around to the sides.

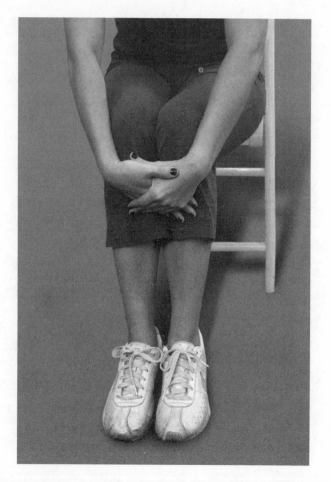

C. Bend forward and place your hands just below the knees, with your thumbs intertwined. With your eyes open, round your upper back until your arms are straight, and look up at the ceiling. Feel a gentle stretch from your hands to your kidney area.

D. Contract your abdomen as you exhale softly, slowly, and evenly
    on the sound *CHOOOO* (breath only; after the initial *ch* sound,
    make the sound of blowing out a candle). As you make the sound,
    visualize any fear, nervousness, constriction, or imbalance leav-
    ing your mouth as a cloudy gray substance that disappears into
    the earth.

E. Bring your hands back to cover your kidneys again, and return your ankles and knees to their first position, comfortably apart. Close your eyes and smile inwardly and outwardly to your kidneys and bladder. Appreciate their crucial work in cleansing your blood, maintaining your water level, and supplying energy to all your internal organs. Continue smiling as you imagine breathing *blue light* into your kidneys and bladder for a total of three or six breaths.

F.   Repeat steps A through E for a total of three or six times. After each sound repetition, return your hands to your kidney area.

After your last repetition, sense that your kidneys and bladder are larger, softer, and moister. Fear, nervousness, constriction, or imbalance have been released. Gentleness, calmness, willpower, and wisdom have increased.

If the season is winter, do double the number of *CHOOOO* sounds.

Sound #3: Anger and Its Variations into Kindness

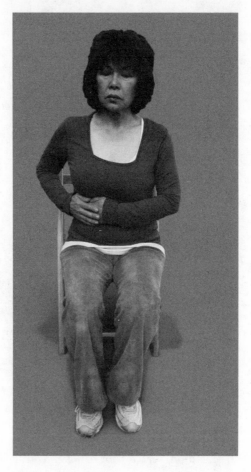

A. Anger and its variations dwell in the liver and gallbladder, whose
season is spring. With closed eyes, connect to your liver and gallbladder by pushing in gently, under your right ribs; you'll feel
your liver there. The gallbladder is below your liver. Sense if
there is any anger, jealousy, resentment, frustration, stress, constriction, or imbalance there. If there is, ask for the message of
this feeling.

B. Open your eyes and inhale deeply and slowly through your nose as you sweep your arms out at each side, and then up.

C. Bring your arms above your head. Interlace your fingers and turn your palms up. Straighten your arms. Press up more on your right arm and lean slightly over to your left. Bend your head back gently and look up. Feel a gentle stretch from your right palm to your liver area.

D. Exhale softly, slowly, and evenly on the sound *SHHHHHH* (breath only, not vocalized), the sound we make to ask for quiet. Visualize any anger, jealousy, resentment, frustration, stress, constriction, or imbalance leaving your mouth as a cloudy gray substance that disappears into the earth to be transformed.

E. Release your fingers and push out with your palms as you sweep your arms down at the sides. Breathe normally.

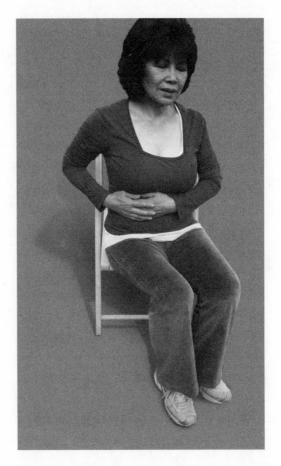

F.   Cover your liver area with your hands. Close your eyes and smile
      to your liver and gallbladder. Appreciate their essential work in
      digestion, regulating blood sugar, and the cleansing of toxins.
      Continue smiling as you imagine breathing a *spring-green light*
      into these organs for a total of three or six breaths.

G. Repeat steps A through E for a total of three or six times. After each sound repetition, return your hands to cover your liver area. After your last repetition, sense that your liver and gallbladder are softer, moister, and larger. Anger, jealousy, resentment, frustration, stress, constriction, or imbalance have been released. Kindness, generosity, decisiveness, planning, and precision have increased.

If the season is spring, do double the number of *SHHHHHH* sounds.

Sound #4: Arrogance into Joy

A. Arrogance and its variations reside in the heart and small intes-
    tine, which are dominant in the summer. Close your eyes and
    connect to your heart. Place your hands on your heart, located in
    the center-left part of your chest; it's a little bigger than your fist.
    See if you feel any impatience, arrogance, mania (overexcite-
    ment), cruelty, hate, constriction, heat, or imbalance there. If so,
    ask for the message of the feeling.

B. The beginning arm movement is the same as for the liver. So
    open your eyes and inhale through the nose as you sweep your
    arms out at each side, and then up.

C. Raise your arms above your head. Interlace your fingers and turn
    your palms up. Tilt your head back and look up. Straighten your
    arms and press up more with your left arm, and lean to the right.
    Feel a gentle stretch from your left palm to your heart area.

D. Exhale slowly, softly, and evenly on the sound *HAWWWWWW* (breath and vocal cords are used). Visualize any arrogance, impatience, mania, cruelty, hate, constriction, heat, or imbalance leaving your mouth as a cloudy gray substance that disappears into the earth.

E.   Release your fingers and push out with your palms as you sweep your arms down at your sides.

F.   Cover your heart with your hands. Close your eyes and smile to
     your heart and small intestine. Appreciate their essential roles in
     circulation, cleansing, nourishment, and digestion. Still smiling,
     imagine breathing a radiant *red light* into these organs with every
     breath, for a total of three or six breaths.

G. Repeat steps A through F for a total of three, six, or nine times. After each sound repetition, return your hands to the chest to cover the heart area.

   After your last repetition, sense that your heart and small intestine are softer, moister, larger, and cooler. Arrogance, impatience, mania, cruelty, hate, constriction, heat, or imbalance have been released. Joy, gratitude, trust, compassion, and love have grown.

   If it's summer, do double the number of *HAWWWWWW* sounds.

Sound #5: Worry into Openness

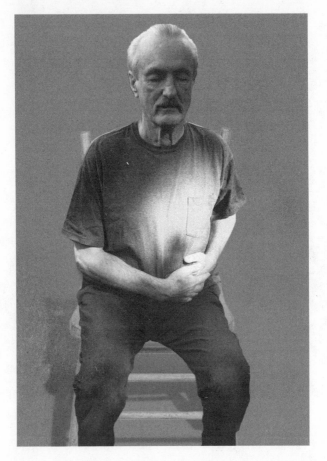

A. Worry and its variations lodge in our stomach, spleen, and pan-
    creas, which are dominant in late summer. Close your eyes and
    place your hands just under your left rib cage. You'll be touching
    your stomach; your pancreas is behind your stomach, and your
    spleen is inside the left ribs. Notice if you feel any worry, anxi-
    ety, shame, self-pity, constriction, or imbalance there. If there is,
    ask for the message of this feeling.

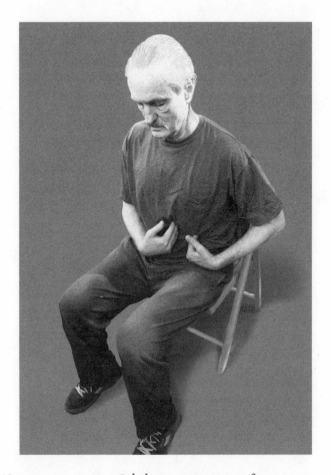

B. Now open your eyes. Inhale as you turn your fingers perpendicular to the floor, and press them gently into your abdomen, just
below the ribs. Place your right hand slightly left of the sternum,
and your left hand in line with the nipple.

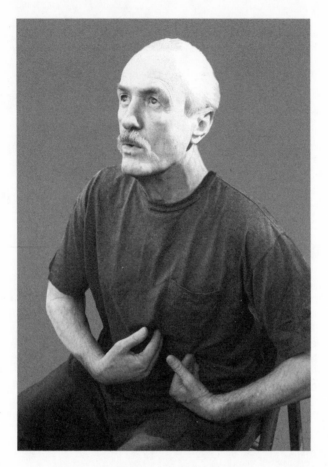

C. Round your back and look up at the ceiling. Exhale softly, slowly, and evenly on the sound *HOOOOOO* (breath and vocal cords). Visualize any worry, anxiety, shame, or self-pity leaving as a cloudy gray substance that disappears into the earth.

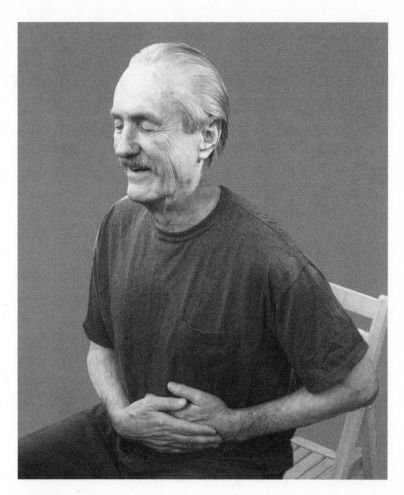

D. Return your hands to below the left rib cage. Close your eyes and smile to your stomach, spleen, and pancreas. Be grateful for their roles in digestion and absorption. Still smiling, breathe normally as you imagine you are breathing *golden yellow light* into these organs, for a total of three or six breaths.

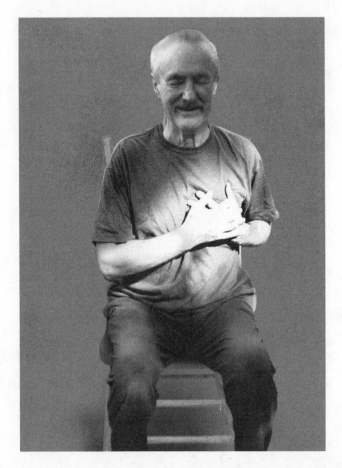

E.   Repeat steps A through D for a total of three or six times. After each sound repetition, return your hands to your abdomen to cover these organs.

After your last repetition, sense that your stomach, spleen, and pancreas are larger, moister, and softer. Worry, anxiety, shame, self-pity, constriction, or imbalance have been released. Openness, fairness, intention, and stability have increased.

If it's late summer, do double the number of *HOOOOOO* sounds.

Sound #6: Stress into Relaxation or Sleep

The last sound is the triple warmer sound. It doesn't relate to a season or color. It evens out the temperature of the three energy centers of the body. The upper warmer covers the area from the head to the bottom of the rib cage; its energy is hot. The middle warmer covers the area from below the rib cage to the navel; its energy is warm. The lower warmer covers the area from the navel to the feet; its energy is cold. Doing the sound makes all three areas warm, which is the ideal body temperature. It also releases stress and induces relaxation. Many Taoist practitioners have cured insomnia by doing all six sounds, with a special emphasis on this one.

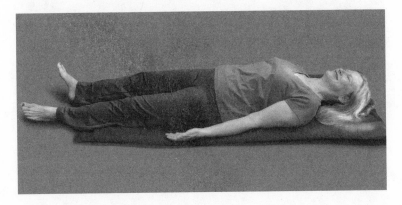

A. If you're doing the sounds just before bedtime, turn off the lights and lie down on your back, under the covers, with your arms by your sides, palms up. If you don't want to fall asleep, lie down on your back on a comfortable surface with your palms up. If you only want to relax, but can't lie down where you are, just lean back comfortably in a chair.

B.   Close your eyes. Move your hands, palms up, to a few inches above your thighs; don't touch your body. Then slowly raise your hands to above your forehead as you take a single deep breath, directing it into your abdomen and allowing the abdomen to expand. Your chest will expand at the same time.

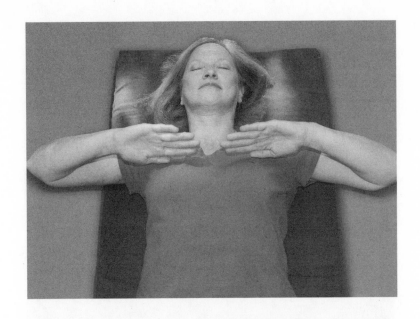

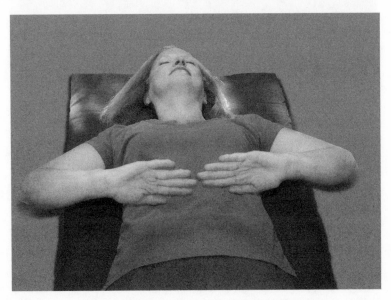

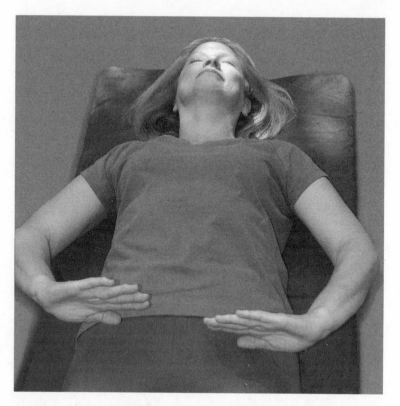

C. Slowly, softly, and evenly, exhale on the sound *HEEEEEE* (breath
    and vocal cords). At the same time, keeping your hands *a few
    inches above your body*, move them down the midline of your
    body. Let your hands and the sound act *as if* they are a roller,
    deflating first your chest, then your solar plexus, then your
    abdomen. Bring your hands back to your sides, palms up. Then
    send the sound into your arms and legs and out through the tips
    of your fingers and toes. Visualize any stress as a cloudy gray
    substance leaving your body and disappearing into the earth.

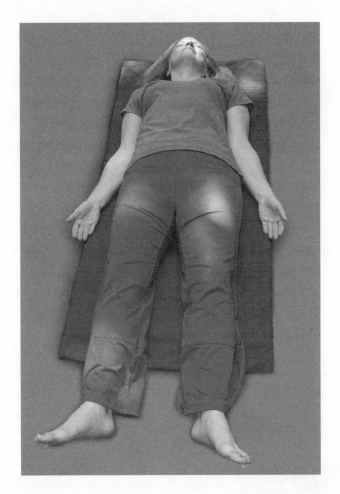

D. Rest and breathe normally as your body temperature becomes evenly warm.

Repeat steps A through D for a total of three or six times or until you fall asleep. After a few sequences, you can just leave your arms by your sides and let the sound alone act as if it is a roller, compressing your chest, solar plexus, and abdomen. If you're doing the sound for relaxation, repeat the steps until you feel calm and peaceful.

A Brief Summary of the Six Healing Sounds

1. Sadness into Courage — Lungs and Large Intestines

Eyes closed. Hands on rib cage. Sense any sadness, depression, constriction, or imbalance in lungs. Ask for its message.

Eyes open. Inhale deeply through the nose as you raise your palms, a few inches out from the body, to above your head. Rotate palms up; leave six inches between them. Head back, elbows bent. Feel stretch from palms to lung area.

Exhale softly, slowly, evenly on *SSSSSS* (breath only), releasing sadness and depression into the earth.

Breathe normally. Rotate palms down. Float hands back to cover ribs. Close eyes and smile to lungs. Breathe in *white light*.

Do all steps three to six times. Do double that number in fall. Cover lungs after each sound repetition. At end, sense that the lungs are softer, moister, spongier. Courage, right action, and letting go have been increased.

2. Fear into Gentleness — Kidneys and Bladder

Eyes closed. Hands on kidneys. Sense fear, nervousness, constriction, or imbalance. Ask for its message.

Open eyes. Knees together. Inhale through nose, sweeping arms around to place fingers below knees, thumbs linked. Bend forward, round back, look up.

Contract abdomen as you exhale on *CHOOOO* (breath only). Release any fear, nervousness, constriction, or imbalance into the earth.

Return hands to kidneys and place legs comfortably apart. Close eyes and smile to kidneys. Breathe in *blue light*.

Do three to six times. Do double this number in winter. After each sound, return hands to kidney area. At end, sense that the kidneys are softer, moister, and larger. Gentleness, calmness, wisdom, and will-power have increased.

3. Anger and Its Variations into Kindness — Liver and Gallbladder

Eyes closed. Hands under right ribs. Sense anger, jealousy, resentment, frustration, stress, constriction, or imbalance. Ask for its message.

Open eyes. Inhale deeply through nose as you sweep arms up at sides.

Arms above head. Palms up and fingers interlaced. Straighten arms and lean to left. Head back.

Exhale on the sound *SHHHHHH* (breath only). Release any anger, jealousy, resentment, frustration, stress, constriction, or imbalance into the earth.

Sweep arms down at sides. Cover liver area with hands.

Eyes closed. Smile to liver. Breathe in *spring-green light*.

Do sequence three to six times. Do double the number in spring. After each sound, return hands to liver area. At end, sense that the liver is softer, moister, and larger. Kindness, generosity, decisiveness, planning, and precision have increased.

4. Arrogance into Joy — Heart and Small Intestine

Eyes closed. Hands on center and left of chest. Sense arrogance, impatience, mania, cruelty, hate, constriction, or imbalance. Ask for its message.

Eyes open. Inhale deeply through nose as you sweep arms up at sides.

Arms above head. Palms up and fingers interlaced. Straighten arms and lean to right. Head back.

Exhale on sound *HAWWWWWW* (vocalized). Release any arrogance, impatience, mania, cruelty, hate, constriction, heat, or imbalance into the earth.

Sweep arms down at sides. Cover heart with hands.

Eyes closed. Smile to heart. Breathe in *red light*.

Do sequence three to six times. Do double that number in summer. After each sound, return hands to heart area. At end, sense that the heart is softer, moister, larger, and cooler. Joy, gratitude, trust, compassion, and love have grown.

5. Worry into Openness — Stomach, Spleen, and Pancreas

Eyes closed. Palms under left ribs. Sense worry, anxiety, shame, self-pity, constriction, or imbalance in stomach, spleen, or pancreas. Ask for its message.

Eyes open. Inhale deeply through nose and press in gently below left ribs with fingers perpendicular. Round back and look up. Exhale on the sound *HOOOOOO*. Release any worry, anxiety, shame, self-pity, constriction, or imbalance into the earth.

Eyes closed. Fingers perpendicular under left ribs. Smile to stomach, spleen, pancreas. Breathe in *golden yellow light*.

Do sequence three to six times. Do double that number in late summer. After each sound, return fingers to press in below left ribs. At end, sense that these organs are softer, moister, and larger. Fairness, openness, stability, and intention have grown.

6. Stress into Relaxation or Sleep

Lie down with palms up. Eyes closed.

Inhale deeply through nose to abdomen as you raise hands a few inches above the body to forehead.

Exhale slowly on the sound *HEEEEEE* (vocalized) as you move your palms, just above your body, back down to your sides. Let the sound and hands act *as if* they are a roller, compressing chest and then abdomen. Send the sound down your arms and legs, and out the tips of your fingers and toes, releasing any stress into the earth.

Do sequence three to six times. Continue doing until you reach a relaxed state or fall asleep.

SIX HEALING SOUNDS CHART

Emotions and Qualities	Organs Yin/Yang	Sound	Color/Sense Organ	Tissue/TCM Function	Season/ Element	Direction/ Taste
Sadness, depression / Courage, right action, letting go	Lungs / Large intestine	SSSSSS breath only	White / Nose	Skin, throat, vocal cords, body hair / Rules chi and respiration, spreads fluids & protective chi	Autumn / Metal	West / Spicy
Fear, nervousness / Gentleness, calmness, willpower, wisdom	Kidneys / Bladder, sexual organs	CHOOOO breath only	Blue / Ears	Adrenals, bones, teeth, head hair, lower back, knees, ankles, feet / Sex drive, stores Essence	Winter / Water	North / Salty
Anger, jealousy, frustration, resentment, stress / Kindness, generosity, decisiveness, planning, precision	Liver / Gallbladder	SHHHHHH breath only	Green / Eyes	Nails, tendons, ligaments, small muscles to joints / Stores and regulates volume of blood needed, ensures smooth flow of chi	Spring / Wood	East / Sour
Arrogance, impatience, mania, cruelty, hate / Joy, trust, love, gratitude, compassion	Heart / Small intestine	HAWWWWWW vocalized	Red / Tongue	Taste, sweat, complexion / Controls blood, blood vessels, speech, houses Original Spirit and Mind, rules organs	Summer / Fire	South / Bitter
Worry, anxiety, shame, guilt, self-pity / Fairness, openness, stability, intention	Stomach / Spleen, Pancreas	HOOOOOO vocalized	Golden yellow / Mouth, Lips	Arms, legs, large muscles / Digestion: turns food, drink into chi, transports chi to organs	Late Summer / Earth	Center / Sweet
Peacefulness, relaxation, deep sleep	Triple Warmer 3 Body Areas	HEEEEEE vocalized	—	—	—	—

Part Four

THE INNER SMILE

CHAPTER 11

SMILE POWER

How It Works

IN THE SIX HEALING SOUNDS PRACTICE, we smiled into five major organ pairs. In the Inner Smile, we deepen our smile energy and mentally direct it into all the major organs and glands, the brain and spine, and the autonomic nervous system.

The power of a genuine smile is undeniable. When a baby or a small child smiles at us with delight, we feel blessed. When our energy is low or we're clinging to painful emotions, a spontaneous smile, even from a passing stranger, lifts our spirits and our energy.

Even smiling mechanically, without any emotion, raises our energy. Try this experiment: Close your eyes. Now smile automatically, without any emotion, by raising the corners of your mouth. Notice how your body feels. Next frown automatically, without emotion, by turning down the corners of your mouth. Notice how your body feels. Once more, turn up the corners of your mouth and note how it feels. Even automatic smiling improves our energy level.

We're not talking about phony smiling, about smiling because we think it's expected of us or it will be advantageous. Phony smiling is dishonest, and the recipient usually knows it's false.

Smiling Leads to Better Chi

Living our lives with habitual tension or turbulent emotions lowers the vibration level of our chi, our life-force energy. Daily practice of the Inner Smile creates a higher vibration: a calm, peaceful, and joyful chi, energy that warms and heals our body, mind, and Spirit.

The ancient Taoists said that Inner Smiling causes the internal organs to produce a honeylike secretion that nourishes the whole body. We can use the Inner Smile to create a sweeter life.

Boosting Self-Esteem

In our competitive, materialistic society, so many people have low self-esteem. They feel inferior to the role models they see in the media, those who are more successful, more renowned, and supposedly more attractive. (Skillful makeup and special lighting can make anyone look more attractive.)

Even accomplished and successful people may have poor self-esteem. In a recent interview, actor Dustin Hoffman revealed that, when he received the American Film Institute Lifetime Achievement Award in 1999 and viewed a film commemorating his many outstanding roles, he had a panic attack, became depressed, and decided to quit acting forever. He added, "I never felt I deserved success." Luckily, his wife persuaded him to see a therapist and work through this problem.[1] It's fairly common for professional actors to be shy in their private lives. Acting a role allows them to hide behind the character they're playing.

Practicing the Inner Smile daily makes us love ourselves more, in a healthy way. It lets us appreciate the miracle of our physical bodies. They're incredibly intelligent and complex. Most of our marvelous body systems function automatically and interact with each other harmoniously — unless we harm them with adverse habits or environments.

The Inner Smile fosters love and gratitude for our bodies, our minds, our emotions, and our Spirits — no matter what imperfections we have. (And we all have imperfections.) We look and feel relaxed and radiant. We're more likely to attract the relationships and circumstances that we desire.

When to Do the Inner Smile

When we're first learning the Inner Smile, it takes twenty to thirty minutes to do it. After we know it by heart, it can take five or ten minutes. It can be practiced any time of the day or night. If we do it early in the morning, it will improve our whole day. If we do it during a midafternoon slump, it will give us a boost. If we do it after a stressful workday, it will relax and refresh us for the evening.

The Inner Smile is remarkable for easing distasteful tasks such as dealing with a difficult person or having to communicate bad news. Doing an Inner Smile just before such challenges can make the outcome more beneficial for everyone involved.

Note

1.   Meg Grant, "Just Dustin," *AARP: The Magazine*, March–April 2009, p. 33.

CHAPTER 12

THE INNER SMILE PRACTICE, STEP-BY-STEP

THIS FIVE- TO TEN-MINUTE PRACTICE will *immediately* lift your spirits. With continued practice, it becomes deeper and more profound, a cherished habit of inner joy. As with the Six Healing Sounds, its power comes from a kinesthetic experience, not a cerebral one. When you're first learning it, it's best to follow the complete instructions below, which acknowledge the specific functions of each of the internal organs. After you've done this for about seven sessions, you can switch to the Brief Summary of the Inner Smile instructions near the end of the chapter, which concentrate on a grateful, smiling connection to each part, rather than on how they work.

Preparation

Wait at least an hour after eating. Allow twenty to thirty minutes for the Inner Smile practice until you know it by heart. Wear loose-fitting, comfortable clothes; natural fabrics allow our chi to flow better. Choose a warm, quiet spot. Dim the lights and turn off the phone. Remove your glasses, jewelry, and watch, and loosen your belt. If you're doing the Inner Smile by itself, it's best to start with the quick standing warm-up described in chapter 10.

Choose a straight-backed chair and put a pillow on the seat for comfort. Sit on the edge of the seat, freeing up the genital area. Keep your legs comfortably apart and your feet solidly on the floor. Relax your shoulders, straighten your back, and bring your chin in slightly. Place your hands on your lap, right hand over left. Close your eyes and breathe naturally.

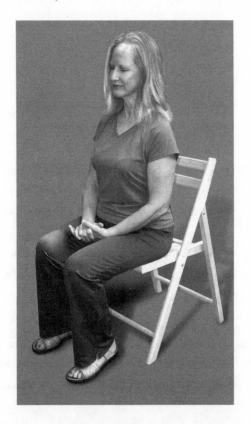

The Front Line: The Major Organs

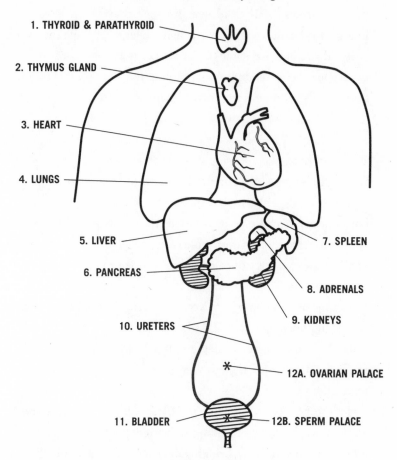

1. **THYROID & PARATHYROID**

2. **THYMUS GLAND**

3. **HEART**

4. **LUNGS**

5. **LIVER**

6. **PANCREAS**

7. **SPLEEN**

8. **ADRENALS**

9. **KIDNEYS**

10. **URETERS**

12A. **OVARIAN PALACE**

11. **BLADDER**

12B. **SPERM PALACE**

FIGURE 12: Inner Smile — The Front Line

1A. Be aware of your feet on the floor, your buttocks on the chair, and your hands in your lap. Relax your forehead. Now, recall an image that makes you smile inwardly and outwardly; it could be the face of someone you love, a joyous occasion, or a beautiful sight in nature. Really see that image in your mind's eye and feel that smiling energy in your actual eyes.

1B. Mentally direct that smiling energy to flow to the point between your eyebrows, your third eye. Imagine the golden Cosmic Energy flowing into your third eye and joining your smile energy. Direct that combined smile–Cosmic Energy to flow down your nose, your cheeks, and into your mouth. Put your tongue up to the roof of your mouth and leave it there for the rest of the practice. (This connects the two major acupuncture meridians, or energy pathways.) Direct the energy to your jaw; smile into it and feel it release any tension that might be there.

1C. Direct the energy to your throat, to your thyroid and parathyroids. Smile to them and thank the thyroid for producing hormones to regulate your metabolism and the growth rate of your cells; thank the parathyroids for producing hormones to regulate the exchange of calcium between your blood and your bones.

2. Direct the smiling energy to your thymus gland. Thank it for furnishing hormones that stimulate production of white blood cells for defense against infection. (Chi kung believes we can reactivate the thymus, though Western medicine believes it atrophies after puberty.)

3. Bring the energy to your heart. Thank it for its constant and essential work in pumping blood at the right pressure to circulate it throughout your body, bringing nutrients, oxygen, antibodies, and hormones to the cells, and removing waste. It never takes a holiday! Thank it for housing Original Spirit, your direct link to Tao.

4. Smile to your lungs. Thank them for their marvelous work in supplying oxygen to all your cells and releasing carbon dioxide.

5. Smile to your liver, the largest organ. Thank it for its amazingly complex work in digestion — processing, storing, and releasing nutrients — and its work in detoxifying harmful substances.

6. Smile to your pancreas. Thank it for producing digestive enzymes, and insulin to regulate blood sugar level.

7. Smile to your spleen. Thank it for deleting worn-out red blood cells, creating white blood cells, and producing antibodies against certain diseases.

8. Smile into your adrenals, on top of the kidneys, and thank them for producing adrenaline for emergencies, as well as producing several other hormones.

9. Smile to your kidneys. Thank them for their excellent work in filtering your blood, excreting waste products, maintaining the water balance of your body, and for producing Essence.

10. Direct the smiling energy back down the kidneys, through the ureters, or tubes, to the bladder and urethra.

11. Thank your bladder for storing and releasing waste liquid (urine) through the urethra.

12. (A) WOMEN: Smile to the ovarian palace, located about three inches below the navel, midway between the ovaries, and an inch inside the body. Smile to your ovaries, uterus, and vagina. Thank your sexual organs for supplying you with hormones and vital sexual energy and for making you the gender you are.

   (B) MEN: Smile to the sperm palace, about one and a half inches above the base of the penis and about one and a half inches inside the body. Smile to the prostate gland, testicles, and penis. Thank your sexual organs for supplying you with hormones and your vital sexual energy and for making you the gender you are.

The Middle Line: The Digestive Tract

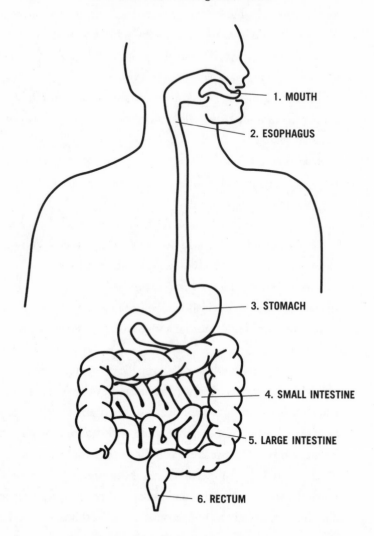

FIGURE 13: Inner Smile — The Middle Line

1. Bring your attention back to your eyes and, once again, see your smiling image and feel its joyful energy. Direct the energy into your mouth. Make a good amount of saliva and swallow it down forcefully and quickly, making a gulping sound.

2. Bring your smiling energy down your esophagus to your stomach.

3. Thank your stomach for liquefying, churning, and partially digesting your food.

4. Direct the smiling energy to your small intestine, which is about twenty feet long in an average adult. Thank it for its incredible work in completing the digestion of your food, absorbing the nutrients into the bloodstream, and releasing the waste products into the large intestine.

5. Smile into your large intestine and thank it for its crucial work in eliminating waste.

6. Smile into your rectum and thank it for releasing waste.

The Back Line: The Brain and Spine

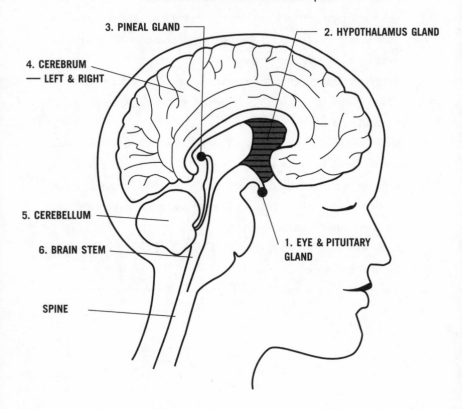

FIGURE 14: Inner Smile — The Back Line: The Brain

1. Bring your attention back to your eyes; see and feel your joyous image. Smile behind your eyes to your pituitary gland. Thank it for producing growth hormone and hormones that stimulate other glands.

2. Above your pituitary, smile into your hypothalamus gland. Thank it for producing hormones to regulate your pituitary gland.

3. Smile behind the hypothalamus to the pineal gland. Thank it for regulating your daily wake/sleep cycle.

4. Smile into the left half of your cerebrum, and thank it for its logical work. Smile into the right half of your cerebrum, and thank it for its intuitive, creative work. Smile into both halves at once, and feel them working together harmoniously.

5. Smile into the cerebellum.

6. Smile into the brain stem.

   (Turn the page to see the illustration of the spine.)

7. Smiling down the spine increases the flow of cerebral spinal fluid and calms the nervous system. Begin to smile down each of the vertebrae of the spine, including the spinal cord inside and the disc, or cushion, below each one. Appreciate the strength and protection of the spine and the nature of the crucial spinal cord. Smile down, counting out each one of the seven cervical, or neck, vertebrae (C1–C7).

8. Smile down each one of the twelve thoracic, or chest, vertebrae (T1–T12).

9. Smile down each one of the five lumbar vertebrae (L1–L5) below the waist.

10. Smile into the sacrum.

11. Smile into the coccyx, or tailbone.

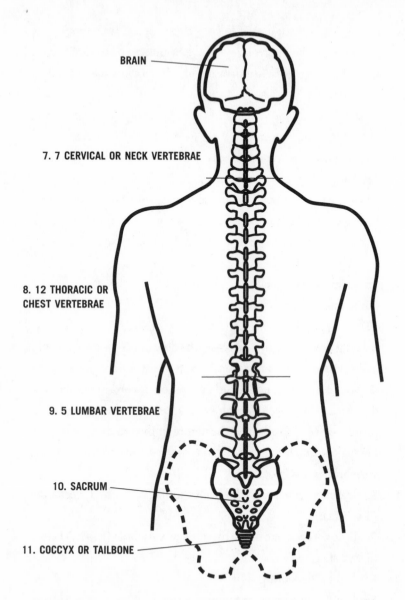

BRAIN

7. 7 CERVICAL OR NECK VERTEBRAE

8. 12 THORACIC OR
CHEST VERTEBRAE

9. 5 LUMBAR VERTEBRAE

10. SACRUM

11. COCCYX OR TAILBONE

FIGURE 15: Inner Smile — The Back Line: The Spine

Smile Down All Three Lines at Once

Return to your eyes and your image that makes you smile inwardly and outwardly. Then go on automatic and smile down all three lines at once; your body now knows how to do this. Then smile into your arms, legs, teeth, nails, skin all over, and hair all over. You are filled with smiling energy, and you know how wonderful you are!

Collect the Energy at the Navel

1. At the end, you must collect and store the energy at the navel. Excess energy in the head or heart can cause severe problems. The navel area can safely handle and store the increased energy. Keep your eyes closed and your tongue up. Direct the smiling energy to your navel and about one inch inside the body. Place your hands over your navel. Spiral your hands around the navel, keeping the spirals below the diaphragm and above the pubic bone.

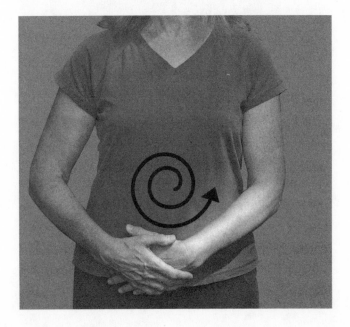

2A. WOMEN: Start spiraling outward from the navel in a counter-clockwise direction thirty-six times; then switch directions and spiral inward, clockwise toward the navel, twenty-four times. Follow the photos for the female direction of the spirals. When you are able to strongly feel the smiling energy, you can spiral the energy mentally.

3. If you feel dizzy or spacey afterward, collect the energy some more by repeating the spiraling in the two directions. You should end up feeling calm, centered, and peaceful.

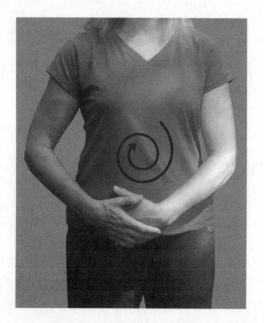

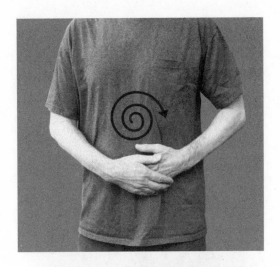

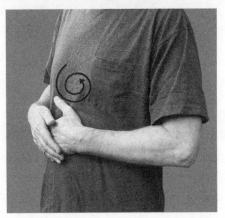

2B. MEN: Spiral this energy outward in a clockwise direction thirty-six times, and then switch directions and spiral inward, counter-clockwise toward the navel, twenty-four times. Follow the photos for the male direction of the spirals. When you are able to strongly feel the smiling energy, you can spiral the energy mentally.

3. If you feel dizzy or spacey afterward, collect the energy some more by repeating the spiraling in the two directions. You should end up feeling calm, centered, and peaceful.

Daily Practice

If you practice the Inner Smile early in the morning, it will improve your whole day. You can also practice it at other times, especially when you feel stress. It takes only five to ten minutes once you know it. If you have muscular pain, smile into the painful area for a few minutes, several times a day. Do the same with any weak areas of your body.

Either immediately or after doing the Inner Smile for a while, your organs will respond noticeably to your appreciation. They may feel warmer or cooler, tingly, and larger. They may even speak to you. "Well, it's about time you thanked me! All these years, you took me for granted!" Being appreciated, they will function even better for you.

A Brief Summary of the Inner Smile Practice

Do the quick standing warm-up in chapter 10. Then sit on the edge of a straight-backed chair with knees and legs comfortably apart and feet on the floor, back straight, chin in slightly. In your lap, place your right hand over the left. Close your eyes, and breathe naturally.

Front Line: The Major Organs

1A. Recall a joyful image and smile inwardly and outwardly.

1B. Direct smiling energy to third eye. Imagine golden Cosmic Energy flowing into third eye and joining smile energy. Smile down into nose, cheeks, and mouth. Put tongue up to roof of mouth and leave there for the entire practice. Smile into jaw and relax it.

1C. Direct smiling energy to throat, into thyroid and parathyroids. Thank them for their excellent work.

2. Smile into thymus gland and thank it.

3. Smile into heart and thank it.

4. Smile into lungs and thank them.

5. Smile into liver and thank it.

6. Smile into pancreas and thank it.

7. Smile into spleen and thank it.

8. Smile into adrenals and thank them.

9. Smile into kidneys and thank them.

10. Smile back down the kidneys and into the ureters and thank them.

11. Smile into the bladder and urethra; thank these organs.

12A. WOMEN: Smile into the ovarian palace, about three inches below navel, one inch inside body, and into ovaries, uterus, and vagina. Thank these for sexual energy and gender.

12B. MEN: Smile into the sperm palace, about one and a half inches above base of penis, about one and a half inches inside body, and into prostate, testicles, and penis. Thank these for sexual energy and gender.

Middle Line: The Digestive Tract

1. Back to eyes: see joyful image again. Smile into mouth and make saliva. Swallow it down forcefully with a gulp.
2. Smile down esophagus and thank it.
3. Smile down esophagus to stomach and thank it.
4. Smile down into small intestine and thank it.
5. Smile into large intestine and thank it.
6. Smile into rectum and thank it.

Back Line: Brain and Spine

1. Back to eyes and joyful image. Smile behind eyes to pituitary gland and thank it.
2. Smile into hypothalamus gland and thank it.
3. Smile into pineal gland and thank it.
4. Smile into left half of cerebrum and thank it. Smile into right half of cerebrum and thank it. Smile into both halves together.
5. Smile into cerebellum and thank it.
6. Smile into brain stem and thank it.
7. Smile to spine: to each vertebra, its disc, and the spinal cord inside. Smile down and thank seven cervical vertebrae.
8. Smile down and thank twelve thoracic vertebrae.
9. Smile down and thank five lumbar vertebrae, below waist.
10. Smile into the sacrum and thank it.
11. Smile into the tailbone, or coccyx, and thank it.

Smile Down All Three Lines at Once

Return to eyes and joyful image. Go on automatic and smile down all three lines at once. Then smile into arms, legs, teeth, nails, skin all over, and hair all over. Filled with smiling energy, know how wonderful you are.

Collect the Energy at the Navel

1. Eyes closed. Hands at navel. Spiral the energy in the area between diaphragm and top of pubic bone.

2A. Women spiral outward from the navel, counterclockwise, thirty-six times. Then spiral inward, clockwise toward the navel, twenty-four times.

2B. Men spiral outward from the navel, clockwise, thirty-six times. Then spiral inward, counterclockwise toward the navel, twenty-four times.

3. Repeat spiraling in both directions if you feel ungrounded or have too much energy in head. You should feel calm and peaceful.

Part Five

RELEASING ONE
RESISTANT EMOTION

CHAPTER 13

THE RELEASING ONE EMOTION PRACTICE

PHYSICAL PAIN IS A SIGNAL OF DISTRESS in the body. Likewise, emotional pain signals distress in the psyche. Regularly doing the Six Healing Sounds and the Inner Smile transforms, balances, and harmonizes all our emotions. However, if we have one or more resistant troubling emotions, we can unblock them with the Releasing One Emotion technique. This method can be done in ten minutes, or you can spend longer if you wish. It acts as a powerful catalyst.

The Releasing One Emotion Practice, Step-by-Step

1. Retreat to a quiet, private space. Start by saying this affirmation (or your own version) out loud: "I forgive myself for not being perfect. It is natural to have negative feelings in some circumstances. I am a very good person. I can learn from and transform my negative feelings. And so it is." Now breathe in through your nose and out through your mouth.

2. Pick one very strong emotion that is troubling you currently. Mentally go back into the situation that elicited this emotion. Let yourself see and hear the particulars: where you were, who was there, the sights and sounds and smells.

3. Allow yourself to feel the depth of the feeling. *Exaggerate it. Become the feeling.* Write about it. Or draw a picture of it. Or scream or shout it out.

4. Now shake your whole body vigorously; literally shake off the painful feeling. Do this for a minute or more. Then take a deep breath to release the pain. Next, say out loud, "I totally release all of this (name of the emotion)."

5. Ask for the message, the lesson, of this feeling. It may come then or some other time during the day, or at a later time. When you receive it, write it down in a journal, give thanks for the lesson, and start acting on the message.

6. Out loud, forgive any other person involved in the emotional situation. Thank him or her for this valuable lesson. Then say out loud, "I release you to your joy and your good, and you release me to mine."

7. Out loud, forgive yourself for your part in this situation.

8. Do three to six repetitions of the Healing Sound for this emotion. Continue working with this same emotion for as many days or weeks as needed, until it can be managed easily with the Six Healing Sounds and the Inner Smile tools.

9. If you have time the same day, proceed through all Six Healing Sounds and the Inner Smile. If not, do it the next day, and alternate between Releasing One Emotion and the Sounds. Add the Inner Smile to your daily routine when you're ready. Continue this process with any feelings that disturb you, addressing one feeling at a time.

Part Six

TAOIST NATURAL FIRST AID
Physical Healing

CHAPTER 14

RELIEVE PHYSICAL SYMPTOMS

An Alphabetical List

MANY MINOR PHYSICAL IMBALANCES can be relieved by doing specific Healing Sounds, the Inner Smile, and Releasing One Emotion. A number of practitioners have used them to cure stress, insomnia, indigestion, overeating, or smoking of cigarettes or marijuana.

CAUTION: *If you have a serious or life-threatening illness, please work with skilled physicians or health practitioners.* No doubt, the techniques in this book can assist your professional treatment by calming and relaxing you. However, *do not rely on these techniques alone.*

The best results for the following problems occur when the suggested practices are supported by moderate exercise, adequate sleep, and three regular nutritious meals each day that include all five tastes and all five colors.

ARTHRITIS: Do nine to eighteen *SHHHHHH* sounds (anger, jealousy). To balance your emotions and internal organs, either then or later in the day, do all Six Healing Sounds three to six times each. Do the Inner Smile every day, smiling more to your liver and heart. Do the Releasing One Emotion practice a few times a week. Emphasize green foods and sour foods in your diet. Include some raw fermented foods daily. Practice being looser and more flexible with yourself and others. Many Western scientific studies show that regular practice of tai chi alleviates arthritis.

ASTHMA: Do the sound *SSSSSS* (sadness, depression) nine to eighteen times. Then or later in the day, do all Six Healing Sounds three to six times each. Do the Inner Smile, and smile more to your lungs and large intestine. Do the Releasing One Emotion practice for sadness and depression. Work on forgiving yourself and others for past mistakes and traumas.

BACKACHE: Do six to eighteen *CHOOOO* sounds (fear, nervousness). Then or later in the day, do all Six Healing Sounds. Do the Inner Smile, and smile more to the kidneys and the area of pain. Hit (gently), massage, and palm kidneys and sacrum six to twelve times. Do stretching exercises; learn tai chi, or Iron Shirt chi kung, or chi kung postures.

BAD BREATH: Do six to eighteen *HOOOOOO* sounds (worry, self-pity, anxiety). Then or later in the day, do all Six Healing Sounds. Do the Inner Smile, and smile more to the stomach, pancreas, and spleen. Bless and appreciate your food. Take small bites, eat slowly, and chew each mouthful until it is liquid.

BODY ODOR: Do the *SSSSSS* and the *CHOOOO* sounds (sadness and fear) six to eighteen times each. Then or later, do all the Healing Sounds in sequence. Do the Inner Smile, and smile more to your lungs and kidneys. Slap your lung area six to nine times. With your fists, gently hit your kidney area. With your palms, massage and warm that area.

COLD OR FLU: Do six to eighteen *SSSSS* sounds (sadness, depression). Then or later, do all the Healing Sounds in sequence. Do the Inner Smile, and smile more to your lungs and large intestine. Slap your lung area. Rest and drink liquids. Fresh lemon juice with hot water and a little cayenne pepper will help clear your nose and lungs.

COLD SORES: Do six to eighteen *HAWWWWWW* sounds (impatience, arrogance). Then or later, do all the Healing Sounds. Do the Inner Smile, and smile more to your mouth, tongue, and heart.

CONSTIPATION: Do six to eighteen *SSSSSS* sounds (sadness, depression). Then or later, do all the Healing Sounds in sequence. Do the Inner Smile, and smile more to your lungs and large intestine. Place one hand over the other and rub your abdomen in thirty-six clockwise circles only, the same direction as the large intestine excretes waste. Eat a raw carrot or banana. Eat some spicy food and food with fiber. Eat some raw fermented foods daily. Do a mild colon cleanse with cooked black or white fungus purchased at a Chinese herb or grocery store or online.

DIARRHEA: Do six to eighteen *HOOOOOO* sounds (worry, self-pity, anxiety). Then or later, do all the Healing Sounds in sequence. Do the Inner Smile, and smile more to your stomach, spleen, and pancreas. Place one hand over the other and rub your abdomen in thirty-six counterclockwise circles only. Eat only rice congee soup until diarrhea stops: cook one cup basmati or white rice with six cups water for a few hours. Eat it plain. When diarrhea improves, add steamed zucchini; after a few more meals, add stewed, peeled apple to meals.

DIZZINESS: Do six to eighteen *CHOOOO* sounds (fear, nervousness). Then or later, do all the Healing Sounds in sequence. Massage the space between the large and small balls of the feet. Eat some grounding food, such as cooked whole grains and beans. Eat something salty; an umeboshi plum is very grounding. Take a nap. Go to bed earlier than usual.

EYE STRAIN; RED, WATERY EYES: Do six to eighteen *SHHHHHH* sounds (anger, jealousy, resentment). Then or later, do all Six Healing Sounds in sequence. Do the Inner Smile, and smile more to the eyes, liver, and gallbladder. Take frequent breaks from your computer or other close work. Alternate close looking with looking into the distance. Get in the habit of blinking often. When reading, move your head along with your eyes as you read each line of printed material.

FATIGUE: Do six to eighteen *SSSSSS* and *CHOOOO* sounds (sadness and fear) at least a few hours before bedtime. Then or later, do all Six Healing Sounds in sequence. Take a nap. Get adequate sleep at night.

HEADACHE: Do six to eighteen *SHHHHHH* sounds (anger, jealousy, resentment). Then or later, do all Six Healing Sounds in sequence. Do the Inner Smile, and smile more to your forehead, liver, and gallbladder. Massage your temples. Massage your scalp with your fingers, *going front to back only, from your hairline back to your neck*. Eat some sour foods.

HIGH BLOOD PRESSURE: This is due to too much energy in the head. Do the first five Healing Sounds six to nine times each, in sequence; then do the *HEEEEEE* sound twice that many times. Massage your feet. Keep your feet warm. After any type of meditation, collect the energy in the navel, following the method given for the Inner Smile.

INDIGESTION: Do six to eighteen *HOOOOOO* sounds (worry, self-pity, anxiety). This is the only sound that can be done immediately after eating. Afterward, wait at least an hour and do all Six Healing Sounds in sequence. Do the Inner Smile, and smile more to your stomach, spleen, and pancreas. Eat three nutritious meals a day on a regular schedule; have your dinner three hours before bedtime. Eat slowly; take small bites and mix each one with lots of saliva and chew it until it's liquid. *Stop eating when you're 80 percent full.* Eat a variety of the five tastes and colors every day. Sweet foods that will benefit your digestion are cooked whole grains (presoaked overnight; see directions in chapter 8), cooked beans (presoaked overnight), cooked sweet potatoes, red potatoes, and squash. We weaken our digestion and our stamina by eating sugar-sweetened food or too many sweet fruits. Switch from cane sugar to a small amount of raw honey or 100 percent pure organic maple syrup. Bitter and spicy foods will also strengthen your digestion. Twenty minutes before a meal, try drinking a half cup of organic wine or filtered water with a few squeezes of fresh lemon added.

INSOMNIA: Do all Six Healing Sounds in sequence. When you come to the *HEEEEEE* sound (relaxation, sleep), turn out the lights, lie down under the covers, and keep doing the sound until you fall asleep. It's important that you don't eat anything later than three hours before bedtime. Do relaxing activities at night — don't watch TV news or violent or disturbing films at night. The *HEEEEEE* sound has helped countless practitioners to cure long-standing insomnia.

MUCOUS: Do six to eighteen *SSSSSS* and *HOOOOOO* sounds (sadness, depression, worry, and anxiety). Do all Six Healing Sounds in sequence. Do the Inner Smile, and smile more to your lungs, stomach, spleen, and pancreas. Avoid cane sugar. Avoid eating a lot of sweet foods. Eat some spicy and bitter foods. Use a neti pot with warm salt water to clean your nasal passages a few times a week.

MUSCLE CRAMPS: Do six to eighteen *HOOOOOO* sounds (worry, anxiety, self-pity). If the cramps are in the legs at night, massage both legs before sleep. Do some gentle stretching exercises or a short tai chi form before bedtime. Do all Six Healing Sounds in sequence, just before bedtime. Learn and practice Iron Shirt chi kung or other chi kung postures. (Do them no later than three hours before bedtime.)

NAUSEA: Do six to eighteen *HOOOOOO* sounds (worry, anxiety, self-pity). When the nausea subsides, do all Six Healing Sounds in sequence. Drink boiled warm water. When you can, eat rice congee soup. See Diarrhea, for the recipe and other food suggestions.

PAIN: Smile frequently into the area of pain. Massage it. Ask for the message of the pain, and act on it. Do the entire Inner Smile practice. Do all Six Healing Sounds in sequence.

SMOKING CESSATION (cigarettes and marijuana): Do six to eighteen *SSSSSS* sounds (sadness, depression, letting go). Do all Six Healing Sounds in sequence. Do the Inner Smile, and smile more to your lungs and heart. Do the Releasing One Emotion practice for sadness, depression, or any other resistant emotions. Eat regular nutritious meals; eat all five tastes and colors daily. Moderate, regular exercise is important. Don't watch TV news at night; don't watch violent or disturbing shows or films. Deep, restful sleep is important. See suggestions under Insomnia.

SORE THROAT: Do six to eighteen *HAWWWWWW* sounds (impatience, arrogance). Do all Six Healing Sounds in sequence. Do the Inner Smile, and smile more to your throat and heart. Drink warm boiled water with fresh lemon juice and raw honey. Rest your voice. Take a nap. Go to bed early.

STRESS: Do six to eighteen *SHHHHHH* and *HEEEEEE* sounds (stress, relaxation, sleep). Do all Six Healing Sounds in sequence. Do the entire Inner Smile practice. Eat calming, cooked, sweet foods such as yams, rice, oatmeal, quinoa, broccoli, carrots, red potatoes, and turnips. Take a walk in a park or in the country. Ignore newspapers and TV news. Take a warm bath. Listen to peaceful classical music. Treat yourself to a massage.

SWOLLEN GUMS: Do six to eighteen *HAWWWWW* sounds (impatience, arrogance, overexcitement). Do all Six Healing Sounds in sequence. Do the Inner Smile, and smile more to the gums and heart.

TOOTHACHE: Do six to eighteen *SSSSS* sounds (sadness, depression). Do all Six Healing Sounds in sequence. Do the Inner Smile, and smile more to your teeth, lungs, and kidneys. Chew on a whole clove or apply a few drops of clove oil.

WEIGHT, EXCESS: Do all Six Healing Sounds in sequence twice a day. Do the Inner Smile before each meal. Do the Releasing One Emotion practice a few times a week for individual resistant emotions. Eat fresh, local organic food *that you enjoy*, and prepare it (or have it prepared) with love and appreciation. Use *fresh* herbs to please your palate. Eat three meals daily, or three smaller meals and two small snacks, on a regular schedule. Eat the last meal three hours before bedtime, and don't eat anything afterward. Eat slowly, savor each bite, and chew it thoroughly until it is liquid. Train yourself to stop eating when you're 80 percent full. Eat a variety of foods, with all of the five tastes and five colors daily. Include one or more raw fermented foods daily. Eat small amounts of raw organic butter. Stir-fry vegetables in water or with raw organic coconut oil. (You need quality fat to lose fat.) For dessert, eat raw organic fruits and nuts (soaked for a few hours). Moderate exercise daily is important. *Find a creative outlet that you care deeply about. Volunteer to help children, adults, or animals in need.*

A WEEKLY PLAN FOR USING THE EMOTIONAL WISDOM TOOLS

THOROUGHLY LEARN AND PRACTICE one of our three wisdom tools for a few weeks. Once you know it by heart and feel the benefits, move on to the next one. When you know and use all three, make a plan you can follow.

The fastest and deepest benefits of the Healing Sounds and Inner Smile come when you integrate them into your daily schedule. Doing the Inner Smile in the morning after exercising and before you start your day's work will improve the quality of your entire day. It can also be done during the day, on a break, or in the evening.

Doing the Six Healing Sounds at bedtime will give you a deep, rejuvenating sleep. They can also be done anytime in the day or evening. Remember to use individual sounds to relieve specific symptoms shown in our Taoist first aid list in the preceding pages. However, keep in mind that doing only sadness sounds or only fear sounds before bedtime may be too energizing. Either do all six sounds before bed, or do these two earlier in the day or evening.

The Releasing One Emotion practice should be worked into your day when you need to focus on one particular aggravating emotion. However, it's best not to do it shortly before bedtime.

SPIRITUAL WISDOM

Dear Reader,
We have shared with you
three Taoist treasures,
ways to learn from and transform
our painful emotions —
those urgings from our Soul
to balance that which
is out of balance.

These powerful tools
can bring us peace and equanimity
in the daily ebb and flow
of challenges and triumphs,
of reflection, activity, and rest.

These tools can remind us:
we are divinely conceived,
tiny but precious beings
of cosmic energy.
We are
the energy of stars and planets.
We are
the magnificent expression
Of Universal Love.

Universal Love
can envision,
Universal Love
can manifest
all that we need:
vibrant health, joyful relationships, abundant supply,
and a gracious manner
that blesses all those whom it touches.

Sustained by this love,
together
we can create
heaven here on earth.

D.S.

SELECTED REFERENCES

Transforming Emotions

Chia, Mantak, with Dena Saxer. *Taoist Ways to Transform Stress into Vitality*. Doi Saket, Chiang Mai, Thailand: Universal Healing Tao Publications, 1985. Out of print in the U.S.

Sankey, Mikio. *Discern the Whisper: Esoteric Acupuncture*. Vol. 2. Inglewood, CA: Mountain Castle Publishing, 2002.

Chi Kung (Qigong)

Chia, Mantak. *Awaken Healing Energy through the Tao*. New York: Aurora Press, 1983.

———. *Iron Shirt Chi Kung I*. Rochester, VT: Inner Traditions, Bear & Co., 2006.

———. *Tao Yin*. Rochester, VT: Inner Traditions, Bear & Co., 2005.

Chia, Mantak, and Maneewan Chia. *Awaken Healing Light of the Tao*. Rochester, VT: Inner Traditions, Bear & Co., 2008.

———. *Fusion of the Five Elements I*. Rochester, VT: Inner Traditions, Bear & Co., 2007.

Chia, Mantak, and Juan Li. *The Inner Structure of Tai Chi*. Rochester, VT: Inner Traditions, Bear & Co., 2005.

Chia, Mantak, with Dena Saxer. *Chi Self-Massage: The Taoist Way of Rejuvenation*. 2nd ed. Rochester, VT: Inner Traditions, Bear & Co., 2006.

Reid, Daniel. *The Tao of Health, Sex, and Longevity*. London: Simon & Schuster, 1996. A valuable comprehensive overview of and guide to Taoist history, philosophy, meditation, exercise, and nutrition by a devoted practitioner.

Lao Tzu's Tao Te Ching in English

Chia, Mantak, and Tao Huang. *Door to All Wonders*. Rochester, VT: Inner Traditions, Bear & Co., 2001. An analysis of *Tao Te Ching* according to esoteric Taoist philosophy, by two chi kung practitioners and teachers. Includes a plain translation of *Tao Te Ching* by Tao Huang with Edward Brennan with some fresh insights. Second edition: *The Secret Teachings of the Tao te Ching*, 2005.

Feng, Gia-Fu, and Jane English. *Lao Tsu: Tao Te Ching*. New York: Vintage Books, 1972. A poetic, clear version with beautiful photos of nature.

Keping, Wang. *The Classic of the Dao: A New Investigation*. Beijing, China: Foreign Languages Press, 1998. A recent, plain translation with extensive interpretations by modern Chinese scholars.

Le Guin, Ursula K. *Lao Tʒu: Tao Te Ching: A Book about the Way and the Power of the Way*. Boston: Shambhala, 1997. A clear, poetic version with passion and humor, featuring helpful paraphrases and intriguing commentaries at the ends of many chapters. Includes both genders as "wise souls."

Waley, Arthur. *The Way and Its Power: A Study of the Tao Te Ching and Its Place in Chinese Thought*. New York: Macmillan, 1956. An elegant, clear version by a Chinese scholar, with helpful paraphrases and commentaries at the ends of most chapters.

Chuang Tzu's Writings

Chuang Tzu. *The Essential Chuang Tʒu*. Translated by Sam Hamill and J. P. Seaton. Boston: Shambhala, 1998.

Feng, Gia-Fu, and Jane English, trans. *Chuang Tsu: Inner Chapters*. New York: Vintage Books, 1974. A clear translation with beautiful photos of nature.

Taoist Philosophy

Kaltenmark, Max. *Lao Tʒu and Taoism*. Stanford, CA: Stanford University Press, 1969.

Ni, Hua Ching. *8000 Years of Wisdom: Conversations with Taoist Master Ni, Hua Ching*. Bk. 1. Los Angeles: College of Tao and Traditional Chinese Healing, 1983.

Traditional Chinese Medicine

Kaptchuk, Ted J. *The Web That Has No Weaver*. New York: Congdon and Weed, 1983. A comprehensive introduction to TCM.

Maciocia, Giovanni, CAc. *The Foundations of Chinese Medicine: A Comprehensive Text for Acupuncturists and Herbalists*. Edinburgh: Churchill Livingstone, 1989. For practitioners and students of TCM.

Reid, Daniel. *The Shambhala Guide to Traditional Chinese Medicine*. Boston: Shambhala, 1996. An excellent brief introduction to a complex system.

Nutrition

Berry, Linda. *Internal Cleansing: Rid Your Body of Toxins and Return to Vibrant Good Health*. Rocklin, CA: Prima Publishing, 1997. Practical, natural methods of cleansing and rebuilding health by a chiropractor, nutritionist, and Taoist instructor.

Fallon, Sally, with Mary G. Enig. *Nourishing Traditions*. 2nd ed. Washington, DC: New Trends Publishing, 2001. An excellent resource combining traditional wisdom and modern scientific findings. Stresses the importance of fermented foods and animal fat, including butter. Includes preparation guides and seven hundred recipes.

Jensen, Bernard. *Foods That Heal*. Garden City Park, New York: Avery Publishing, 1988. A valuable guide to a healthy, natural diet by an

American pioneer in nutrition. Analysis of foods according to their nutrients and therapeutic value.

Katz, Sandor Ellix. *Wild Fermentation: The Flavor, Nutrition, and Craft of Live-Culture Foods*. White River Junction, VT: Chelsea Green, 2003. The best book we know of on fermenting foods. Easy, precise recipes for sauerkraut, yogurt, kefir, bread, kombucha, wine, and other unusual ferments.

Ni, Maoshing. *Secrets of Self-Healing*. New York: Avery, 2008. Healing foods and herbs, acupressure and exercises for wellness and for common ailments.

Ni, Maoshing, with B. S. McNease. *The Tao of Nutrition*. New and expanded ed. Los Angeles: SevenStar Communication Group, 2000. Clear presentation of Taoist nutritional guidelines, benefits of common foods, and dietary remedies.

Pitchford, Paul. *Healing with Whole Foods: Oriental Traditions and Modern Nutrition*. Berkeley, CA: North Atlantic Books, 1993. An excellent and comprehensive reference book for nutrition, including Taoist, Ayurvedic, and Western dietary principles, preparation guides, and over three hundred recipes.

Sankey, Mikio. *Support the Mountain: Nutrition for Expanded Consciousness*. Inglewood, CA: Mountain Castle Publishing, 2008. Combines the Chinese Five Element approach to food with naturopathic medicine and whole, raw foods. Recommends minerals and their foods for each element. Stresses foods that support a higher spiritual vibration.

Taoist Sexology

Chia, Mantak, and Douglas Abrams Arava. *The Multi-Orgasmic Man*. San Francisco: HarperCollins, 1996.

Chia, Mantak, Maneewan Chia, Douglas Abrams, and Rachel Carlton Abrams, M.D. *The Multi-Orgasmic Couple*. San Francisco: HarperCollins, 2002.

Chia, Mantak, and Rachel Carlton Abrams. *The Multi-Orgasmic Woman*. Emmaus, PA: Rodale Publications, 2005.

Chia, Mantak, and Maneewan Chia, with Marcia Kerwit. *Healing Love through the Tao: Cultivating Female Sexual Energy*. Rochester, VT: Inner Traditions, Bear & Co., 2005.

Chia, Mantak, and Michael Winn. *Taoist Secrets of Love: Cultivating Male Sexual Energy*. New York: Aurora Press, 1984.

Modern Science in Sync with Taoist Theory

Capra, Fritjof. *The Tao of Physics*. 2nd ed. Boston: Shambhala New Science Library, 1985.

Gershon, Michael D. *The Second Brain*. New York: HarperCollins, 1998.

Pearsall, Paul. *The Heart's Code*. New York: Broadway Books, 1998.

Pert, Candace B. *Molecules of Emotion: The Science Behind Mind-Body Medicine*. New York: Scribner, 1997.

Ancient Sufi Wisdom

Hafiz. *The Gift: Poems by Hafiz, the Great Sufi Master*. Translated by Daniel Ladinsky. New York: Penguin, 1999.

Rumi, Jelaluddin. *The Essential Rumi*. Translated by Coleman Barks. New York: HarperCollins, 1995.

Modern Spiritual Wisdom

Beesley, Ronald P. *Esoteric Christianity*. Kent, England: White Lodge Publications, 1975. Profound analysis of the roles of Soul and Spirit. Out of print; try esoteric book websites, such as Abebooks, Powell's, or Alibris.

———. *The Path of Esoteric Truthfulness*. Kent, England: White Lodge Publications, 1976. Superb and accessible; excellent understanding of emotions, Soul, and Spirit. Out of print; try esoteric book websites.

———. *Yoga of the Inward Path*. Kent, England: White Lodge Publications, 1974. Available from DeVorss & Company. An invaluable guide to the principles of spiritual development.

Chopra, Deepak. *The Seven Spiritual Laws of Success*. Novato, CA: Amber-Allen Publishing and New World Library, 1993. A clear,

succinct presentation of the basic spiritual laws that lead to fulfill-
ment in all of life.

Emerson, Ralph Waldo. *Self-Reliance*. White Plains, NY: Peter Pauper
Press, 1967. Emerson's philosophy resonates with Taoism.

Hoff, Benjamin. *The Tao of Pooh*. New York: Dutton, 1982. A wise and
delightful presentation of Taoism, as practiced by the ultimate Taoist
sage, Winnie-the-Pooh.

Ming-Dao, Deng. *365 Tao*. San Francisco: HarperSanFrancisco, 1992.
Beautiful, intriguing poems and insights for every day of the year.

Tolle, Eckhart. *The Power of Now: A Guide to Spiritual Enlightenment*.
Novato, CA: New World Library, 1997. Inspiring, clearly presented
guidelines for grounding one's body, for emotional release, and for
evolving spiritually.

Human Anatomy

Memmler, Ruth Lundeen, and Dena Lin Wood. *Structure and Function of
the Human Body*. 3rd ed. Philadelphia: Lippincott, 1983.

ACKNOWLEDGMENTS

Mantak Chia

MY DEEP GRATITUDE TO ALL THOSE MEN AND WOMEN who helped and supported me in writing this book. In particular, I give thanks:

To the countless generations of Taoist sages who formulated and refined the natural practices in this book for healing and harnessing negative emotions.

To my major Taoist teacher, Yi Eng, for his openness and vision in teaching me the Inner Alchemy of the Taoist practices and in authorizing and inspiring me to bring them to the Western world.

To all the senior instructors of the Universal Healing Tao System worldwide who have helped me enrich and clarify the teaching of the Taoist practices. To all the certified instructors of the Universal Healing Tao System worldwide who continue to share this knowledge with their students. To all devoted teachers, physicians, and practitioners of the Taoist healing arts.

To Doug Abrams of Idea Architects for seeing the need for this book, for guiding us in writing the proposal, and for selling it to New World Library.

To our editors at New World Library: Jason Gardner, for his keen interest and overall guidance, and Bonita Hurd, for her quality, detailed editing. To all the other NWL specialists who have so ably assisted us.

To my coauthor, Dena Saxer, for her personal insights into the value and meaning of negative emotions. For her clear, skillful writing style and diligent research. For her nutritional suggestions and her dedication to this book.

To the staff of Universal Healing Tao Publications, especially Leck (Monsuda Suyasaroj) and Jim (Suthisa Chaisarn), who ably assisted with communications between myself — while in Thailand and elsewhere in the world — and Dena in California.

To my dear parents, now deceased, for their love and support and for encouraging my interest in meditation and martial arts.

To my beloved son, Max, and his dear wife, Wim, for the love and joy they give me.

To Tao, the origin of All.

ACKNOWLEDGMENTS

Dena Saxer

MY SINCERE THANKS TO ALL THOSE WHO HELPED to make this book a reality. In particular, I give thanks:

To those ancient Taoist men and women who discovered how to transform emotional pain.

To Mantak Chia for teaching me his modern synthesis of the ancient practices, for certifying me as a senior instructor, and for inviting me to cowrite this book and two previous ones. The Taoist practices have enhanced every aspect of my life, and I am forever grateful to him.

To Doug Abrams of Idea Architects, who suggested we write this book, recommended its basic focus, edited the proposal, and promptly sold it to New World Library.

To Jason Gardner, senior editor at New World Library, for his enthusiastic support and his superb, incisive, and crucial suggestions.

To our copy editor, Bonita Hurd, for her outstanding detailed editing, and for leaving no stone of vagueness unturned. To all the other first-rate professionals at NWL who have helped us, especially artist and designer Tracy Pitts, type designer Tona Pearce Myers, and publicist Kim Corbin.

To our photograph artist, Fae Horowitz, who captured not just the images but also the energy of the Healing Sounds and Inner Smile.

To my kind students who generously posed for the photos in the book: Ellen Palame, Jessica Cope, Yoshi Russo, Cheming Martinez, John Coolick, and Anne Lingua. To all my dear students who made the techniques in this book their own and gave me fresh insight into them.

To Captain Campbell Line of Toronto, now deceased, my first dowsing teacher, who introduced me to energy work. To Ronald P. Beesley, now deceased, founder of the College of Psychotherapeutics, in England, for the profound spiritual teachings presented in his books.

To my first Universal Healing Tao teachers, Rylin Malone Weil, now deceased, and Gunther Weil, who opened the gate for this journey. To my UHT buddies, Marcia Kerwit and Raven Cohan, for their wisdom and humor.

To Trish Shannon, now deceased, Rod Menzies, Debra Ann Robinson, Randall Gates, Patri Gouzy, Tina Alleguez, and Max Perkoff for their excellent suggestions and ready encouragement. To Ken Wong for his invaluable editing of the drawings. To my buddies who cheered me on: Roz Harris, Joan Jason, Susi Oak, and Erick Aguirre, and to Sara Goren, now deceased.

To my darling mother, Anne Cohen, recently deceased, who inspired and encouraged my love for the arts and my humanistic beliefs. To my beloved father, Rubin Saxer, who, though he died when I was twelve, inspired and supported my joy in creating and my love for nature. To my dear stepbrother, Ben Goldman, and stepsister-in-law Janie Goldman, who is now deceased, for nurturing and inspiring me as a teenager. To my dear aunt, Lillian Levine, for her love and kindness.

To my marvelous children, Ruth and David, for teaching me how to love and, with their spouses, for being dedicated and joyful parents. To Ruth's dear spouse, Doug, and their children, Jessica, Matthew, Tara, and Brendan. To David's dear spouse, Gayle, and their children, Jacob, Sara, and Jarid. I thank you all for the countless blessings you bring me.

To Tao, the Source of all.

INDEX

D

daily practice
 Inner Smile and, 170
 Six Healing Sounds and, 98
 weekly planner and, 189–90
dairy products, 55
dampness, 85
death, acceptance of, 35, 39–40
decisiveness and planning, 63, 65
Defensive chi, 44
defensiveness, anger and, 61
depression. *See* sadness and depression
detachment, 34–35, 40–41
diagnosable mental disorders, prevalence of, xiii
diarrhea, 183
digestion, 46
 large intestine and, 43
 relieving indigestion, 185
 Six Healing Sounds and, 100
 small intestine and, 74
 stomach, spleen, and pancreas, 84, 88
 water consumption and, 56
digestive tract, Inner Smile and, *162*, 162–63
discernment, 75
disease
 genetically modified foods and, 46
 relieving physical symptoms, 181–88
 sadness and depression, 44–45
 Traditional Chinese Medicine (TCM) and, xv–xvi, xix
 See also physical problems
divine origins, Taoism and, 10–11
divorce, 41
dizziness, 184

E

Earth energy, 18, 19, 20, 85, 91
Earth Force, 13, 14–15
ego, meditation and, 29
Elements, Five, 17–21
Emotional Chi, 12
emotional disharmony, xv
emotional healing
 negative emotions and, 11
 Releasing One Emotion and, xix
 Six Healing Sounds and, xvii–xviii
 timeframe for, 5

emotions
 anger, 59–67
 arrogance, impatience, cruelty, hate, and mania, 69–77
 energy (*chi*) and, xv, xvi
 fear and nervousness, 49–57
 negative emotions and, xiv
 organ functions and, xviii
 sadness and depression, 39–48
 Six Healing Sounds and, 99
 value of, 3–6
 worry, anxiety, shame, guilt, and self-pity, 79–91
energy (*chi*)
 emotions and, xv, xvi
 energy imbalances, 14–15
 Inner Smile and, 153, 154, 167–69
 lungs and, 44
 meditation and, 29
 Six Healing Sounds and, 97
 Taoism and, 12–15
 worry, anxiety, shame, guilt, and self-pity, 80
 yin and yang, 15–17, 17–23
energy collection, Inner Smile and, 167–69, 173
energy, external, *13*, 13
 Three Pure Ones, 13
energy, internal, 12
Enig, Mary, 87
Essence, 52, 53
The Essential Chuang Tzu, 8
Ethereal Soul, 65
evolution of the self, 11–12, 20–21
excellence, Taoism and, 33
exercise, 98, 186, 188
excessive compulsion, 65
expanding energy, 17
external energy, 12, *13*, 13–15
eyes, Inner Smile and, 160, 163, 165, 171, 172
eye strain, 184

F

failure, sadness, and depression and, 40
Fallon, Sally, 87
fall season, 109, 115
fatigue, 184
fear and nervousness
 arrogance, impatience, cruelty, hate, and mania, 72

ABOUT MANTAK CHIA

MANTAK CHIA IS THE LEADING TEACHER of Taoist chi kung (Inner Alchemy, Sexual Alchemy, chi energy meditations, tai chi, chi kung, etc.) in the West. The author of dozens of books, booklets, DVDs, and CDs describing the theory and methods of these practices, Mantak Chia has taught hundreds of thousands of eager students the principles of Taoist Inner Alchemy practice over the past forty-five years. He is the creator of the Universal Healing Tao System, which distills and clarifies the Taoist practices, and the director of the Tao Garden Health Spa and Resort in Thailand. Taught by over twelve hundred certified instructors and practitioners on every continent, the Universal Healing Tao System provides access to a uniquely modern integration of traditional theory, method, and practice.

The Universal Healing Tao System is a practical system of self-cultivation and independent spiritual development. Mantak Chia created the system to effectively share the many ancient Chinese meditative and internal energy practices transmitted to him by a series of masters and teachers throughout Asia. His sincere wish is that every individual might have the opportunity to complete the harmonious evolution of body, mind, and

Spirit. Through these practices, the student learns to take personal responsibility for his or her own physical, emotional, and spiritual well-being.

Mantak Chia was born in Thailand to Chinese parents in 1944. Recognized very early as having great potential for spiritual development, he was initiated into meditation practices by Buddhist monks at the age of six. While studying in Hong Kong, he learned tai chi chuan, aikido, and kundalini yoga from a variety of teachers. His pursuit of Taoist teachings led him, at age fifteen, to meet Yi Eng (White Cloud Hermit), a Taoist master originally from central China, who was living at that time in the mountains not far from Hong Kong.

Eventually Yi Eng was to become Mantak Chia's principal teacher. Over a period of ten years, Yi transmitted to Mantak Chia the most sacred and closely held Taoist practices, formulas, and methods of internal alchemy. Realizing that, as transmitted to him, these important practices could not easily be absorbed by Western students, Mantak Chia undertook to clarify and demystify them and to integrate them with his studies in Western human anatomy.

Mantak Chia lived for fifteen years in New York before returning to Thailand in 1994. He now spends much of the year traveling in Europe, the United States, Asia, Africa, and South America, leading workshops and giving lectures.

Currently, Universal Healing Tao Centers exist in cities across the United States and in Canada, Mexico, Brazil, Denmark, Austria, Belgium, Cyprus, England, France, Germany, Greece, Ireland, Italy, the Netherlands, Russia, Scotland, Spain, Sweden, Switzerland, Turkey, Wales, Australia, New Zealand, China, Israel, Japan, Malaysia, Thailand, the Philippines, Singapore, and South Africa.

Visit Mantak Chia's website at
www.universal-tao.com.

Visit the Tao Garden Health Spa and Resort website at
www.tao-garden.com.

ABOUT DENA SAXER

DENA SAXER IS A SENIOR INSTRUCTOR of Mantak Chia's Universal Healing Tao System of chi kung. She sees these teachings as a precious gift to the world. Since 1983, she has been practicing and teaching the Six Healing Sounds, Inner Smile, advanced Taoist meditations, tai chi chi kung, and Iron Shirt chi kung. Several thousand adults ages eighteen to seventy have benefited from her caring, dynamic, and clear teaching style.

With Mantak Chia, she cowrote *Taoist Ways to Transform Stress into Vitality* in 1985 and *Chi Self-Massage* in 1986. Both books have been translated into more than twenty languages worldwide.

Residing in the mountains near Los Angeles, Dena teaches Universal Healing Tao classes there, as well as in other locations worldwide. She is a trained dowser, and she specializes in energy clearing for homes and properties. She also does private sessions of spiritual and emotional healing.

Dena's other hat is that of writer: she writes plays, lyrics, and librettos for the theater. She's a member of the Alliance of Los Angeles Playwrights. Her drama *Kathe Kollwitz: A Dangerous Act* was produced by Theatre

Imago in Santa Monica, California. She cowrote a comedy revue, *My Fair Bag Lady*, produced in Toronto, and two comedy sketches for CBC Radio. She has cowritten a musical drama and a musical comedy with composer Gordon Glor. She is currently working on a feature film script.

Graduating from Wayne State University in Detroit, Dena received an MA in theater and speech education. For eleven years, along with teaching Taoist classes, she taught public speaking and interpersonal communication in the Los Angeles Community Colleges to several thousand working adults from diverse cultures. She started each class with a few of the Healing Sounds, and her students loved this routine; it helped them to calm down and concentrate after a hectic workday.

For ten years in Toronto, Dena was a professional actor. She performed leading and supporting roles at the Stratford Shakespearean Festival and on CBC TV and Radio, as well as in several documentary films.

Dena is blessed with a wonderful daughter and son, their equally wonderful spouses, and seven unique and delightful grandchildren.

Visit Dena Saxer's website at
www.universaltaola.com.

To find a certified Universal Healing Tao instructor
in your area, go to http://directoryofuniversaltaoinstructors.com/.